COPYRIGHT AND DEVELOPMENT: INEQUALITY IN THE INFORMATION AGE

Edited by
Philip G. Altbach

Bellagio Studies in Publishing, 4

Bellagio Publishing Network
Research and Information Center
in association with the Boston College
Center for International Higher Education

Bellagio Publishing Network publications are distributed by
the African Books Collective, Ltd.

January 1995
Second printing, March, 1996

© 1995 Bellagio Publishing Network

Copies of this book may be ordered from
African Books Collective, Ltd.
The Jam Factory
27 Park End St.
Oxford OX1 1HU, UK
Fax: 44-1865-793298

ISBN number: 0-937033-58-8
(CIP information available from the Library of Congress)

Bellagio Studies in Publishing, 4

Other titles in this series include:

1: Philip G. Altbach, editor, *Publishing in Africa and the Third World*

2: Carol Priestley, *Publishing Assistance Programs: Review and Inventory*

3: Philip G. Altbach and Hyaeweol Choi, *Bibliography on Publishing in the Third World, 1980-1993*   (Published by Ablex Publishers, 355 Chestnut St., Norwood, NJ 07648 USA)

4: Philip G. Altbach, editor, *Copyright and Development: Inequality in the Information Age*

5: Urvashi Butalia and Ritu Menon, *Making a Difference: Feminist Publishing in the South*

6: Henry M. Chakava, *Publishing in Africa: One Man's Perspective*

TABLE OF CONTENTS

About the Bellagio Publishing Network

The Bellagio Publishing Network is an informal association of organizations dedicated to the strengthening of indigenous publishing in the Third World. The groups include publishers, donor organizations from both government and private voluntary sectors and others concerned with publishing and book development. Established in 1991, the Bellagio Publishing Network has focused its attention on promoting indigenous publishing in Africa. It has provided a forum for discussion as well as a collaborative network for assisting publishing and book development activities.

The Research and Information Center of the Bellagio Publishing Network assists the Network by providing information and sponsoring research related to book development and publishing. It publishes the *Bellagio Publishing Network Newsletter*, a quarterly focusing on Third World publishing. The center also sponsors research and information gathering activities designed to improve the knowledge base on Third World publishing and providing data and analysis that will provide direct help to publishers and to others concerned with book development. The Research and Information Center is funded through a grant from the Rockefeller Foundation. It is a part of the research and service activities of the International Center for Jesuit Higher Education at Boston College.

Further information can be obtained from the Center, 226 Campion Hall, Boston College, Chestnut Hill, Massachusetts 02167, USA. FAX: (617) 552-8422.

The Bellagio Publishing Network Secretariat is located at The Jam Factory, 27 Park End St., Oxford OX1 1HU, England. FAX (44) 865 793-298.

INTRODUCTION

Copyright and Development fills an important void in the current debate about copyright. Copyright is now universally accepted—if not always practiced. This is a remarkable changes from just a few decades ago, when many countries did not subscribe to the international copyright treaties and some in the Third World argued vociferously against copyright on the basis that it kept knowledge from those who needed it most. Now, everyone agrees that the international knowledge system must have rules to guide it and regulations are necessary. The pendulum has swung toward copyright as an important idea. Indeed, in some ways it has swung too far. Those who "own" knowledge, the copyright holders, now have all of the advantages. Courts routinely rule in their favor and the various international treaties, such as the General Agreement on Tariffs and Trade (GATT), enshrine the idea of intellectual property. The owners are now able to almost completely control knowledge products. This book tries to bring some balance to the debate. All of the contributors agree that copyright is important—but most feel that there must be access to information as well as control of information. The authors here disagree on a number of points, but all are united by a conviction that copyright must be understood in a complex international environment. We hope that these essays will stimulate discussion not only concerning the control of knowledge and intellectual property, but also about the responsibilities that owners as well as users have to ensure the dissemination of knowledge.

Copyright and Development is the fourth in a series sponsored by the Research and Information of the Bellagio Publishing Network. The Network is concerned with fostering indigenous publishing in the developing countries of the Third World and especially in Africa. The Research Program, of which this publication is a part, is intended to build up understanding of issues relating to publishing and book development. The Bellagio Publishing Network is funded by the Rockefeller Foundation, and is part of the research and service program of the Boston College International Resource Center for Jesuit Higher Education.

I am indebted to the authors of the essays in this book. All are busy professionals in the field of publishing. Their commitment not only to publishing books but also to understanding the complex issues relating to contemporary publishing is appreciated. James J.F. Forest and Gabriel Altbach assisted in the editing and formatting.

Philip G. Altbach
Chestnut Hill, Massachusetts
January 1995

Chapter 1

THE SUBTLE INEQUALITIES OF COPYRIGHT

Philip G. Altbach

Copyright is well entrenched in international publishing, and yet it faces significant challenges. On the surface, copyright has never been stronger. The concept is increasingly accepted worldwide, and even those Third World countries, such as India, that argued against the inequalities of the international copyright system in the 1960s have largely ceased their opposition. Even China has joined the international copyright system. While piracy has not ended, it has gone underground in all but a few countries. Massive pressure from the United States and Britain has brought such former pirates as Korea, Taiwan, and Singapore into the fold. Perhaps most important, the concept of copyright is almost universally accepted by governments and by those involved in the book trade worldwide.

Copyright has been strengthened by strong governmental pressure from the major publishing countries and from the legal systems in these countries. Copyright has been seen as much as a means of protecting trade advantages as it has as a basic concept of knowledge distribution. The United States and Britain have been concerned about the loss of 'knowledge products' of all kinds (of which books are now only a minor part) because these losses contribute to ever-growing negative trade balances.

The fact is that the printed word, which is the concern of this essay, has been lost in the campaign to protect profits on computer software, compact disks, films, and other products is a problem for both publishers and readers, since books and journals present special circumstances that require attention. Further, the courts have been increasingly zealous in their protection of copyright and the prerogatives of the owners of knowledge products. For example, in the United States, the courts have narrowly construed copyright regulations in favor of publishers and against those who have claimed 'fair use' in reproducing materials for academic purposes.

These rulings have significantly increased the power of copyright owners.

GATT and Intellectual Property

The recently completed negotiations over GATT (General Agreement on Tariffs and Trade) has further entrenched copyright and has created a new means of litigation and control, the World Trade Organization. Intellectual property is a central part of GATT, and GATT enforcement arrangements now join those of the Berne Convention and the Universal Copyright Convention. The products of the mind are considered as commercial property, to be bought and sold in the marketplace. Few see any difference between knowledge products and any other commodity. GATT enshrines the idea that those who bring knowledge products to the marketplace should be able to completely control them.

It is time to take a step back from rampant commercialism to examine the complex world of copyright and the distribution of knowledge. There is, in reality, a difference between a Mickey Mouse watch, a Hollywood film, or even a computer software program, on the one hand, and a scientific treatise, on the other. Textbooks, technical reports, and research volumes are subject to the same copyright regulations as a novel by James Clavell. Those who control the distribution of knowledge treat all intellectual property equally—and are perfectly happy to deny access to anyone who cannot pay. The legal structures set up to protect intellectual property benefit the owners. There is no consideration of the user. The attitude seems to be: No pay, no play.

But even in the marketplace of intellectual property, there was room for negotiation during the GATT deliberations. The French successfully argued that there should be limitations on the free flow of American cultural products to Europe because of a fear of inundation by Disney and Rambo. The French had influence, and a compromise was reached. There are, thus, some "non-market" restrictions allowed in GATT. But no such compromises were permitted for those countries that depend on knowledge products from the industrialized nations and cannot afford to pay the going rates for them. There are no provisions in place to ensure that developing countries can have access to books and other knowledge products.

As it stands, GATT is a blunt instrument which will inevitably work to the disadvantage of poor nations in terms of access to knowledge. Modifications in the current straitjacket imposed by GATT and by the copyright treaties do not mean a rejection of free trade or the idea of a global market-based economy.

Technological Challenges

Yet, all is not secure in this era of narrowly construed copyright. Perhaps the greatest challenge to traditional copyright is technology. Every new technological advance brings a flurry of litigation and efforts by copyright owners to limit access to new technologies until their rights can be fully protected. A recent example of this was the fight over digital audio tape (DAT) technology. The widespread dissemination of DAT was held up for several years while the producers of DAT machines and the owners of copyright (mainly the recording companies) struggled over how to ensure that copyright owners would be protected. Photocopiers have posed a continuing challenge to copyright owners and, while the courts have consistently ruled in favor of the publishers, the battle lines are forever changing as new and more sophisticated reprographic technologies are introduced. Data networks are also a new area of contention for copyright holders. How can knowledge products be controlled in an era of instantaneous communication through computer-based networks?

Currently, the most perplexing issues relate to computer programs, computer-based communications networks such as the Internet, and related technological spin-offs. Owners, in this case software companies, data base operators and the like, are concerned that the ownership of such innovative technologies be clear, and that non sanctioned use be prohibited and punished where it occurs. Trade related intellectual property (TRIPS) has been among the most debated topics in the GATT negotiations. While books and other traditional knowledge products are hardly at the frontier of technology, they have been swept up in the campaign to strengthen ownership.

Recent Debates

It is significant that these battles are over technological innovations. The debate over copyright principles raged in the

1960s and 1970s over issues relating to the appropriateness of control over knowledge and what responsibilities the rich countries had to help build up the educational and scientific systems of the newly developing nations of the Third World. Few argued for the abolition of copyright but many felt that knowledge should be shared more freely and that the industrialized nations, in part because of their earlier colonial domination of the Third World, had special responsibility to assist in the process of development. Some charged the industrialized countries with purposely maintaining tight control over knowledge products in order to keep the Third World in a dependent relationship and to maximize profits. In the ideologically charged Cold War era, charges of neocolonialism were leveled against the major Western countries, and many argued that Western policies were aimed at continuing domination rather than assistance. UNESCO, through its advocacy of a 'new world information order,' weighed in on the side of the Third World critics, enraging Western governments and contributing to the withdrawal of the United States and Britain from the organization.

It was said, for example, that Western publishers preferred to export relatively small numbers of books to the Third World rather than grant reprint rights because more profits could be obtained from direct exports. Some claimed that the foreign aid programs of such countries as France, Britain and the United States were aimed at exporting books and ideas rather than at encouraging indigenous development in Third World countries.

The vociferousness of the debates has abated, but the issues remain important. Most realized that the issues were not mainly ideological in nature and are highly complex. India, one of the main critics of the traditional copyright system, found itself emerging as a major producer of books and, not wanting to harm its future export markets, shifted its posture on copyright issues. Most realized that anarchy in the knowledge business would serve no one's long-term interests and that a workable copyright system is necessary and international cooperation a good idea. With the slow winding down of the cold war, most realized the slogans could not change reality. Countries that stood outside the copyright system, including the Soviet Union and China, slowly joined it.

Patterns of Inequality

Yet, it is important to realize that the international knowledge system is highly unequal, and it can be argued that those who are in control of the system—and specifically copyright arrangements—have a special responsibility to assist in the intellectual and educational development of the Third World. There is a kind of OPEC of knowledge in which a few rich nations and a small number of multinational publishers have a great deal of control over how and where books are published, the prices of printed materials, and the nature of international exchange of knowledge. These same forces tend to dominate the new information and knowledge dissemination technologies. Because the knowledge infrastructures are located in these countries, there is a kind of monopoly that has been difficult to break. And because knowledge is not a finite natural resource but is infinitely expandable, there is the possibility of more countries becoming members of the cartel. There has, in fact, been relatively little expansion in the number of knowledge producing countries—and the price of entry into the cartel increases as the cost and complexity of knowledge production goes up.

Copyright, from its beginnings in England in the sixteenth century, has been a means of protecting the "haves"—of limiting access to books and information in order to maintain order and discipline in the trade—of creating a monopoly over knowledge. There are, of course, very good arguments in favor of copyright. These include the principle that those who create and disseminate knowledge and knowledge products should economically benefit from these creations and that the creator should maintain some basic control over the creation. Also inherent in the idea of copyright is that intellectual creativity should also benefit society—this is indeed the underpinning of copyright as expressed in the American Constitution.

The Responsibility of Copyright

Along with power, and copyright bestows considerable power on the copyright holder, comes responsibility. For the most part, those who hold most of the world's copyrights and who also control the international copyright system have been largely concerned with power—with maintaining control over their copyrights and with maximizing their economic benefits. Copyright is seen in purely legal and economic terms. There is virtually no recognition that there are inherent noneconomic factors involved in copyright and that those who hold power now have a responsibility to assist those who do not have access to the world's knowledge. Copyright, after all, is a moral and ideological concept as well as a legal and economic one. There is no recognition that the legacy of colonialism and the power of the multinationals has, to a significant extent, created the current highly unequal world knowledge system. It is, of course, much easier for the "haves" to cling to the economic and legal underpinnings of a system that has given them a virtual monopoly over the world's knowledge products than to recognize that we live in an interdependent world and that the Third World desperately needs access to knowledge and technology. In the current context, it is unlikely that those who need access to knowledge most will be able to obtain it "at current market rates" any time soon. What is needed now is affirmative action to ensure that books and other knowledge products are not kept from Third World nations because of the restrictions of the copyright system. Copyright holders must now spend time thinking about the needs of Third World readers in addition to their concerns about maintaining market share. In the broader scheme of things, providing the assistance that is needed to the Third World will not cost very much. Indeed, in terms of copyright, the main requirement is largely access to permissions, rights, and a very small amount of market share.

A necessary first step is increased consciousness of the complex issues relating to the world's knowledge system and the role of copyright in it and a recognition that a broader perspective is needed. A modest amount of economic sacrifice may also be required along with some inconvenience. Copyright must not be seen in isolation from issues of access to knowledge, the needs of Third World nations, and the broad history of colonialism and exploitation. It is not productive to point fingers or assess blame for past inequities. Rather, we must quickly move toward copyright arrangements that will maintain the copyright system while at the same time permit flexibility so that the needs of the "have nots" can be met.

The needs are indeed great—and they are not limited to the

poor countries of the developing world. For example, Moscow's famed Lenin Library is no longer purchasing any scientific journals from the West because there is no allocation of 'hard currency' funds. Few, if any, other libraries or academic institutions in the · former Soviet Union are able to obtain access to key books and journals in the current circumstances. The situation is even more desperate for many sub-Saharan African countries, where purchases of books and journals from abroad ceased several years ago because of lack of funds. Some countries lack the facilities to produce many kinds of books and must rely on supplies from abroad. These countries, and the number is depressingly long, are probably in more desperate need now than a decade ago. The end of conflicts in such countries as Cambodia, Laos, Uganda, Angola, Ethiopia, and others has permitted them to turn their attention to the rebuilding of educational and library systems—and there is a desperate need for books of all kinds as well as for the equipment and expertise to build up indigenous publishing capacity. Economic crisis throughout Africa has created special needs—exacerbated in some ways by the emergence of fledgling democratic regimes in some countries that must improve the lives of their citizens if they are to survive. Books are a small but highly visible way of making such improvements. Further, access to knowledge may help to build up a commitment to democratic ideals. Countries in the former Soviet Bloc, from Mongolia and Vietnam, to the Czech Republic and Bulgaria, need speedy access to the world's knowledge, having been cut off from much of it for almost a half-century.

The specific needs vary greatly. In some cases, access to scientific journals and books at subsidized prices for a limited period would help greatly. In others, local publishers with limited markets need easy and inexpensive access to foreign books in order to translate them into the local language. In a different context, permission to reprint books from the industrialized countries in the original language is needed to serve an indigenous population literate in English or French but unable to pay the high cost of imported books. And for some countries, most of the elements of an indigenous publishing industry are missing and there is a need to build it up from scratch. Copyright may not be the key element in all of these circumstances, but it does play a role.

Responsible world citizenship with regard to copyright is unlikely to be extraordinarily costly. Countries and publishers that require special assistance on copyright issues are unlikely to be major customers in any case—markets tend to be small and purchasing power very limited. Yet, there will be some costs involved. Export sales may be modestly reduced and income from the sale of rights foregone or limited. There may also be some administrative costs for industrialized country publishers. But the long-term benefits might well outweigh the immediate costs and inconvenience. A self-sufficient book industry in a Third World country is likely to be a better partner, and in the long term a better customer as well, than would a weak and demoralized publishing community. Further, as the Indian case has shown, self-sufficient publishers tend to be supporters of copyright because they see adherence to copyright in their best interest.

It may be worth recalling that copyright compliance comes naturally with economic and social development. One of the most egregious violators of copyright in the nineteenth century was the United States, which felt, probably incorrectly, that it could build up its domestic publishing industry most effectively by freely reprinting works from abroad while protecting the rights of domestic authors. Once American publishing was well developed, the United States became a defender of copyright. Until the 1960s, the Soviet Union had a similar perspective—international copyright was violated as the country used knowledge from abroad for its own purposes. China has had a similar perspective up to the 1990s and has only recently joined the international copyright system. Nations must see copyright as in their best national interests before then become fully supportive of it.

What Can Be Done?

There are a number of steps that can be taken to help developing countries gain access to the world's knowledge and also build up their own indigenous publishing industries. None require a violation of the basic principles of copyright and, in the long run, will strengthen it because more countries will see it in their best interest to support copyright.

There must be a recognition that all knowledge products are not the same, and that while it may be justified to insist on commercial terms for Nintendo games, some flexibility for scientific materials, textbooks and the like is appropriate. The owners of knowledge must modify their purely profit-oriented approach to certain segments of the knowledge industry.

Permissiveness in copyright relations in the short run may yield more profits in the long run for owners. For example, a publisher may obtain less money by licensing a book for a local edition in Africa or a translation in Asia than by exporting copies. In the long run, however, a viable domestic publishing industry and a literate public will buy ever increasing numbers of books.

The idea of compulsory licensing—providing to Third World countries the automatic right under some very limited circumstances to reprint or translate Western books with the payment of reduced fees—was pressed by Third World representatives at international copyright meetings but never formally ratified by the major international treaties. The concept is a sound one so long as it is kept within carefully limited guidelines. Compulsory licensing would permit Third World publishers quick access to relevant educational and scientific materials by permitting them to reprint or translate materials for educational and a few other uses. The Third World publisher would be required to inform the copyright holder and provide some payment—often at below-market rates. This arrangement removes much of the bureaucracy from the system and also permits Third World readers to have access to knowledge from abroad fairly quickly. One of the common complaints from Third World publishers is that many Western publishers simply do not respond to requests for reprint or translation rights. Charging fees that are clearly beyond the ability of Third World publishers to pay is another common problem.

In the past decade, the copyright "powers" have used every means available to ensure strict compliance with both the spirit and the letter of international copyright treaties and with national copyright laws. One of the most successful tactics used to ensure copyright compliance has been to link it to broader trade arrangements. American copyright holders, for example, have pressured their government to threaten countries who do not enforce copyright with the withdrawal of trade preferences. These threats had a role in convincing such major U.S. trading partners as Taiwan and Singapore to cease most pirating. China is currently facing severe trade sanctions by the United States because of its refusal to cease pirating computer software, CDs, and related products. GATT has further linked copyright to the world trade system. While these efforts have yielded some results in terms of immediate compliance, it can be argued that copyright must be "sold" on its own merits, that it is as much a moral issue as a commercial one, and that making copyright hostage to international trade, an arena where Third World nations have little leverage in any case, is in the long run detrimental to the emergence of a copyright system based on consensus and mutual understanding.

Western publishers must take a long-term view of world publishing. This means their policies must permit offering inexpensive access to books and journals for reprinting and translation. There is a feeling in the Third World that Western publishers often simply ignore the requests of Third World publishers and institutions because there is little money to be made and discussions often become complex and sometimes acrimonious. Western publishers must respond positively and quickly to requests and understand the problems faced by Third World publishers.

Joint ventures or cooperative arrangements with indigenous publishers in the Third World may help both sides. The Western publisher provides expertise, products, and sometimes capital. In return, access to markets is opened up. Such ventures must be on the basis of equality, and autonomy for Third World partners is important. There are many kinds of joint ventures, ranging from a major involvement to cooperation on specific projects. Many involve work together on issues relating to copyright.

The book trade relationships between the industrialized nations and the Third World are unequal. Books are exported from the West to the Third World. Copyright permissions are requested by Third World publishers and are sometimes granted by counterparts in the West. There is very little traffic in the other direction. It may be possible to significantly increase the import of books from developing countries and thus strengthen Third World publishers significantly. It may also be possible for Western publishers to obtain rights to Third World books for publication and distribution in the West. Because most of the world's books are published in the major industrialized countries, the unequal relationship will continue, but there may ways of ameliorating it to a modest extent. It is important to keep in mind that what is a modest transaction to a Western publisher may be a significant development to a Third World firm.

Conclusion

Copyright is, in a way, symbolic of the relations between the 'haves' and 'have nots' in publishing. All of the cards are in the hands of the Western publishers. They control the international copyright treaties, which were, after all, established by them and with their interests in mind. The Western publishers dominate the world book trade. The powerful multinational publishers, which are Western controlled, reach into many countries. In the Reagan-Thatcher era, Western governments have played the 'trade' card to ensure compliance with copyright and patent regulations. While the major beneficiaries have been software producers, film companies and the like, book publishers have also benefited and have strongly supported these initiatives. Copyright is widely respected internationally and, at least for books, is more tightly enforced than has been the case in the past.

The time has come to recognize that the production of books and journals is more than a business, and that trade in knowledge and knowledge products is somehow different than commerce in automobiles or coconuts. Those who control knowledge distribution have a responsibility to ensure that knowledge is available throughout the world at a price that can be afforded by the Third World. I am not advocating overthrowing the copyright system, or even weakening it. I am arguing for a broader understanding of the responsibilities of publishers in a complex and unequal world. Such an understanding will, no doubt, require some rethinking of the relationships between the knowledge 'haves' and 'have nots.' In an era of interdependence, this is not an altogether bad thing. It is likely to be controversial and perhaps unpopular. No one with power likes to share it. But if the immense challenges of Third World development are to be solved, publishers will have to play a modest role.

This is a revised and expanded version of an article that appeared in *Logos* 3 (No. 3, 1992).

Chapter 2

INTERNATIONAL COPYRIGHT AND AFRICA: THE UNEQUAL EXCHANGE

Henry M. Chakava

The recently concluded Rights *Indaba*[1], which coincided with the 1994 Zimbabwe International Book Fair in Harare, brought into the spotlight the thorny issue of Africa and international copyright. The conference had been originally organized as a means of promoting book trade among African states. In the end, it turned out to be a training session with European publishers educating their African colleagues on how best to sell rights into international markets. In spite of reports to the contrary, it is unlikely that the conference achieved its prime objective of increasing trade in rights nor indeed the original one of increasing cross-border trade among the African publishers themselves. The speakers from the North advised African publishers that, in order to make their rights offers more attractive to foreign buyers, they should surrender as much territory as possible. For example, a Zimbabwe publisher should retain only Zimbabwe, and release the rest of the market to the foreign buyer. They were advised not to insist on too high a royalty—7 was recommended as acceptable— and should curb their tendency to ask for too high an advance, because African books are difficult to sell in the North. Above all, they were urged to improve on the quality and presentation of their products and improve their promotion and marketing strategies before, during and after publication of their books. Other somewhat patronizing bits of advice were offered and one got the impression that African publishers were now being called upon to abandon their principal aim of serving their own markets and concentrate on satisfying the needs of foreign rights buyers.

The printed word still remains the easiest, cheapest and most versatile method of communicating and distributing knowledge. The book, in particular, is handy, presentable, easy to store, and readily adaptable to dissemination, retrieval, and transfer of knowledge, in whole or in part. With widespread use of radio and television, coupled with recent advances in the information industry such as video, reprography, computer networking and other innovations facilitating fast transfer of information such as fax, electronic mail, Internet, etc., it was feared that the role of the book and printing technology in general, would decline. This may be the case in some countries but, on the whole, it would appear that the book has not only stood its ground but has again come in handy in the use, application and promotion of these new technologies. Today, the position of the book remains central to the dissemination of knowledge and that reality is unlikely to change in the foreseeable future, especially in Africa. In addition, although it is probably the slowest, most "primitive," and most demanding method of transferring knowledge, the book remains the most effective, in spite of the fact that it does not carry any compensating features.[2]

In this essay, we shall not discuss international copyright per se, or whether or not it serves the interests of justice and equity. We shall merely observe that trade in copyright makes sense only when applied to two equal or almost equal partners, who buy as much as they sell from each other. If one has little or nothing to sell, one administers copyright only in the interests of those who have it. Yet it has to be accepted that international copyright is necessary, even inevitable, if intellectual property is to be protected, its distribution controlled, and those responsible for its creation rewarded and acknowledged for their work. This must be accepted as crucial in shaping and improving the quality of life on a more permanent and long-lasting basis. We shall argue that unless international copyright is administered in a manner which facilitates the sharing of the world's intellectual property and not as a tool of capitalistic selfishness and protectionism, the developing world should regard it with suspicion and should not subscribe to it without certain safeguards and assurances. It is not accidental that some of the world's largest book producers today, such as the former Soviet Union, do not yet subscribe to international copyright. Additionally, today's major book giants, among them the United States, Japan, and China, did not agree to the Berne Convention and its various protocols until they had developed strong national book industries of their own. What promise then does international copyright hold out for Africa, given the fact that 34 out of its 54 countries are members of the Berne Convention?[3] Before we attempt to answer this question, let us take a survey of the available literature on this subject to see if it can illuminate our discussion.

The Literature on Copyright

Most of the literature available on the market, some of which is listed in the bibliography at the end of this essay, does not question or critically examine international copyright, and its positive or negative effects on the world knowledge industry. It merely sets out to explain the law and how it is being enforced, and with what results. A plethora of publications contain advice on how to draw up publishing agreements to cover the variety of rights subsisting in a publication as seen largely from the point of view of the publisher in the North.

The International Publishers Association (IPA), the Scientific Technical Medical Publishers Association (STM), the World Intellectual Property Organization (WIPO), the International Federation of Reproduction Rights Organizations (IFRRO), the mushrooming national reproduction rights organizations (RROs), and national publishing associations in the North, contain up to-date information on copyright: which countries have signed and which are about to sign the various conventions and protocols governing its use—from Florence, the Universal Copyright Convention, to Berne, culminating in their Paris accords, and all the other protocols that have followed. The activities of the various watchdog institutions policing copyright receive constant coverage, as are the new structures being set up especially in the developing world, for this purpose. The manner and extent of copyright infringement, where and when, is constantly highlighted complete with damages that have been paid or imposed, and what new devices are being developed to deal with piracy and what these organizations are doing to cope with the ever-increasing list of threats brought about by the new technologies. Needless to add, this information is essentially for the benefit and in the interest of the North, and Africa receives a mention only when a new African country signs or ratifies these agreements. Philip Altbach's *The Knowledge Context: Comparative Perspectives on the Distribution of Knowledge*[4] *is* one book which adopts an analytical and critical approach similar to the one posited in this essay.

Aims

This essay seeks to bring out and comment upon the social and economic impact of international copyright as it affects the developing world today, to assess the effects of this on the distribution of knowledge. Moreover, it is crucial to define how the present copyright relationship makes possible or hinders the sharing and transfer of knowledge between the North and the South. More specifically, an attempt is made to examine the relevance or irrelevance of international copyright in as far as the present realities of publishing practice in Africa are concerned— what problems or constraints prevent it from exploiting these provisions in order to bring about the free flow of information from North to South, and vice-versa. We shall look briefly at the future of the printed word in a rapidly changing world and extrapolate on the extent to which international copyright can continue to maintain the central and strategic role in the world knowledge industry today and whether it has the capacity, the will and resources to "tame" and control the ever-mushrooming new technologies which are constantly threatening its administration. Finally, while subscribing to the view that international copyright is necessary, we shall conclude by making a few proposals aimed at "humanizing" it in order to make it more responsive to the needs and knowledge requirements of the developing world in general, and Africa in particular.

The Reality: Africa's Output—An Analysis

The reality in Africa, as in the rest of the world today, is that more and more countries are promulgating laws governing national copyright and signing and/or ratifying international, copyright treaties, and in some countries enforcement is being incorporated into national statutes. Some countries have set up or are in the process of setting up RRO's to protect copyright and guard against piracy, not only in the area of publishing but also in such other areas as music performance, reprography and Public Library Rights (PLR). International agencies, especially WIPO and IFRRO, are busy providing technical and financial assistance in the drafting, administration and enforcement of these laws, offering training where it is needed.

The success of these lobbies can be seen in the fact that to-date, according to available data, 106 countries, including China, India, Taiwan, and Germany, have become members of the Berne Convention. The United States, after years of membership only in the UCC, has also joined Berne. Others, such as Russia, North and South Korea are reported to be positively responding to pressure to join. Out of the 106 members mentioned above, 34 are from Africa and constitute nearly one third of the total membership of the Berne Convention[5], leaving only 24 of the remaining African states out but likely to join in the near future. The reasons why African countries have signed these conventions are difficult to understand. The 1993 UNESCO Statistical Year Book[6] shows that although Africa has 12% of the world's population, it produces only 1.2% of its books, and that this percentage is declining. Comparatively, Europe produces 53% of the world's books, compared to Asia (27%) and North America (13%). The situation is no different with newspapers, magazines, journals and other reading materials and they have already taken a commanding lead in the development of the new technologies referred to above. In his book, Altbach observes that 80% of the world's knowledge industries are based in the North and their output is copyrighted there. This means that African countries have signed these protocols, not to protect their own knowledge industries, but to ensure that their people do not use or abuse other peoples' rights.

There seems to be little or no difference in the publishing fortunes or destiny of those countries who have signed copyright agreements, and those who have not. For example, Tanzania was not a signatory until very recently, yet its publishing industry remains one of the least developed in Africa. Neighboring Kenya has a fairly well developed industry yet this cannot be attributed to the fact that it was one of the early signatories to these conventions. Moreover, a lack of publishing capacity, resources, and training makes it difficult to say whether it is Africa's adherence to international copyright or its lack of capacity that has prevented it from engaging in unlawful reprinting, photocopying and pirating of copyrightable materials. We do not know of any African state or publisher who has willfully contravened international copyright as was the case in Asia especially between the 1950s and the 1980s, although we are aware that there has been pirating of books from Asia to West Africa, especially Nigeria.

A closer look at the list of the other states that belong to the Berne Convention shows that these are countries with highly developed publishing industries with a major interest to protect. As we have already observed, major book powers such as the United States, Japan, India and China delayed signing and ratifying these conventions until they had something to offer the world. One can only assume that African countries have chosen to sign because they believe this will facilitate the flow of knowledge from the North to their own countries. What compensation or reparation can Africa get from the North for this bold act of chivalry? Indeed, if this is so, we shall argue that this view still makes sense only in the short run and only if there is co-operation from rights holders in the North, but the reality of the situation is that these rights holders do not appear keen to extend printing licenses to African publishers. Instead they are using copyright as a weapon to maintain the dependency relations that currently exist. The African signatories have arrogated themselves the role of collecting copyright fees from their own people and remitting these to the owners in the North. This has serious repercussions for the cost of education, and for the future of education industries in Africa. When Africa finally gets to Professor Minowa's "take-off" point[8] when the necessary economic, production and distribution infrastructures will be in place and the market sufficiently developed to permit proper commercial publishing to emerge, this is when the magnanimous gesture of the majority of its member states will catch up with this reality. It will find that its hands are tied, and that is when it will replace Asia as the battleground for piracy and other copyright infringement battles presently raging in the rest of the world. For now, lack of capacity and throughput resulting primarily from poverty renders the issue of which countries are signatories and which are not somewhat academic.

Africa has Little to Offer ...

Even if copyright laws were to be administered equitably, and in Africa's best interest, Africa would find that it has little or nothing to sell to the outside world. Its textbooks, which constitute nearly 90% of its total output, can hardly travel within national boundaries, let alone outside Africa. As a matter of fact, a large proportion of these textbooks are published by European publishers or their African branches so that, essentially, the copyright in these works is held by publishers in the North.

The remaining 10% of Africa's book output is made up of liturgical materials, children's books, fiction, academic books and gray literature. The liturgical materials include the standard Bible, hymn books, and bible stories mainly in African languages published by mission presses controlled by the centers of world religions, most of them based in the North. Its children's books are few and not produced to a quality level that can attract foreign interest. Inadequate production expertise and lack of investment finance, and imprudent minimization of risk has led to poor production, marketing and distribution strategies and encouraged excessive reliance on textbook publishing which enjoys a ready market. Academic books are few and are mostly published out of the continent anyway, as is most of the fiction.

Africa's leading fiction writers are published in the North, mostly in Britain, France and the United States. The majority of them sprang into prominence in the 1950's and 1960's when the African publishing industry was either at its nascent stage, or did not exist at all. They continue to be published in those centers partly because local African industries are not yet sufficiently developed to provide maximum exposure to their works, or because they are still bound by contractual obligations to their original publishers. Most publishers in the North have a clause in all their contracts which reads as follows: "The publishers shall have the first refusal of the author's next two works suitable for publication for the educational market (and the author shall offer to the publishers for this purpose the same rights and territories as those covered by this agreement) on terms to be mutually agreed...," a Catch 22 clause which is self-perpetuating. If UNESCO's report that Africa produces 1.2% of the world's books is true, then it would appear that the continent controls only about 0.4% of the world's intellectual property, a sad reality for the 34 African countries that subscribe to the Berne Convention and constitute the largest bloc of members from any continent.

Take the issue of research for example. Most African countries do not have the institutional structures, resources or expertise to engage in research. Most of the research is undertaken by scholars from the North, whose findings are published and copyrighted in the North. It would be foolish to halt essential research for this reason and, as we shall argue in the concluding section of this essay, the solution is to 'humanize' international copyright, both in principle and practice, so that it does not remain a selfish tool in the hands of the rich North. One research area which reveals a glaring contradiction is African oral literatures and traditions which cannot be claimed to be the intellectual property of anybody in particular. Yet, as soon as this is researched into, and the material compiled and published by the researcher (most of them are from the North), it becomes his copyright, and no one can use it without his permission. A few African countries have made certain exceptions about oral literatures and traditions in their national copyright laws, but it does not pay for them to behave like a dog in a manger, and research into these areas is in the interest of scholarship and must go on. Moreover, we should not, as we are doing, accuse publishers in the North of hoarding copyright when we ourselves are placing restrictions on our own intellectual property, for it can be said that oral literature is the vehicle for the exchange of information for about 75% of the entire population of Africa.

We have argued that in spite of having signed and ratified international copyright instruments, African publishers have little or nothing to offer in the facilitation of the free flow of knowledge between nations, one of the cardinal assumptions of international copyright. They are too poor and have little capacity and no experience in the buying and selling of rights. Their foreign counterparts frequently take advantage of them on the few occasions that they engage in such transactions, taking the whole territory when they buy and restricting them to their home ground when they sell. We have also argued that existing copyright watchdogs, whether policed by international agencies such as WIPO, IFRRO or national RRO's, are not focused towards preventing copyright infringement in African published works, thus allowing publishers in the North to take advantage of this situation and to freely flout the very laws that they apply to safeguard their interests in the South. Further we have argued that although the publishing situation in Africa is improving, the present trend is likely to continue for a while yet, as we do not yet foresee a situation in the near future whereby research in Africa will be controlled by African governments and scholars. We have cautioned that the area of oral literatures and traditions is particularly vulnerable, and although several African governments have declared that area to be in the public domain, the majority of scholars who carry out research in it continue to copyright their findings. We shall now see what the North has to offer and establish the extent to which international copyright is a facilitator or a hindrance in the knowledge transfer process between the North and the South.

The North has Everything to Offer, But, ...

As we have already noted, there is little publishing activity taking place in Africa. One way of speeding up the knowledge transfer process is for the publishers in the North to grant reprint licenses to their African counterparts to facilitate faster and cheaper production, and stimulate capacity building. However, experience over the last 30 years has shown that these publishers would rather set up local branches in Africa, or sell directly from the metropole than grant licenses. They are particularly reluctant to sub-license school textbooks even to those countries which have capacity to manufacture them locally. It cannot be argued that they make less profit when they sell rights since in cases where such rights are granted, they would normally insist on a maximum royalty of 20% (which goes into their books "below the line"), yet the majority do not net that kind of profit in their normal publishing operations. We can only surmise that the real reason is selfish and protectionist—they do not want to transfer capacity and the skills that go with its development.

We have also stated that international copyright protects the haves, not the have nots, and is structured to serve the interests of those with something to protect. This was clearly demonstrated in a recent copyright case[9] in the High Court of Kenya where a British multinational publisher sued a local Kenyan publisher for breach of copyright in a Kiswahili[10] novel which had not been re-issued for eight years, but which had suddenly come into prominence by being prescribed for the local "O" level Literature examination. In spite of the existence of a new contract signed between the local author and publisher, and while not disputing the fact that the book had been out of print for that period, the Judge[11] ruled in favor of the British publisher, arguing that as the author had not repossessed his rights from the original publisher, expressly in writing, he had nothing to sell to the Kenyan publisher. As the author had died in the meantime, it was not possible to have him in court to testify, but, even then, the judge did not listen to any witnesses and insisted that without a release letter from the British publisher, the local publisher and his author did not have a foot to stand on. This clearly demonstrates that international copyright is titled towards the interests of metropolitan publishers who use the letter of the law to ensure that rights do not revert to their rightful owners even when they themselves are not in a position to fully exploit them. Other cases have been reported whereby European publishers maintain the minimum stock levels of works by African authors as stipulated in the author-publisher contract, refusing to release them for sale, so that, technically, the work remains in print and they retain copyright until another opportunity to exploit them arises. Unless a provision is made in international copyright conventions to discourage and even punish hoarding of copyright in these and other ways, publishers in the North will continue to use it to deny the developing world of essential knowledge material vital to its development.

In the few exceptional cases where European publishers grant rights to their African counterparts, this is usually done on harsh and unfavorable terms. The license normally covers one printing only, specifying the print-run, but with provision for the grantee to re-negotiate a new reprint which, if granted, is then covered by a fresh contract. The license restricts the territory to the country of the publisher's domicile, so that a Kenyan publisher granted such a license cannot sell his licensed books in neighboring "common" market territories such as Uganda and Tanzania. The royalty demanded is usually between 15 and 20 percent, and where foreign exchange permits, this payment is required to be paid up front on publication, and/or a sizable advance and offset fees are insisted upon in the contract license and must be paid before the license can come into force. Additionally, the African publisher is required to print in one of the preliminary pages of his edition words to the effect that "This reprint has been authorized by (name of publisher) for sale in (name of territory/country) only and not for export therefrom..." Some British rights holders will even insist on having a say in the pricing of the licensed book, the printers to use and the trade discounts to give to certain of their favored booksellers and distributors in the African publisher's territory.

Yet, in the cases where the European publisher is buying rights from an African publisher, he is the one who determines the terms, as was so clearly described at the Harare *Indaba*. The African publisher must retain only his own territory, and must offer the rest to the buyer. In addition, the buyer must be granted all subsidiary rights, including translation rights. The seller should ask for a royalty of 5%, certainly not more than 7%, and should request only a "nominal" advance, if any. If possible, the contract should not carry any time limitation but if it does, a minimum of 5 years, renewable, was recommended. When the book is eventually published, often the foreign publisher does not acknowledge the original African publisher anywhere in the book, and will sometimes claim in his blurb and publicity material that the author is "a new discovery."

As we can see, rights holders in the North want to cling to their rights as tightly as possible, whether they are buying or selling and if and when they decide to buy or sell, they prefer to maintain a North-South vertical axis which cannot facilitate intra-African trade, as each state or publisher is made to sign a separate contract with the foreign publisher on the same title in the same region. The African states themselves are already resigned to this manner of trading with their erstwhile colonial masters, and as books constitute an infinitesimal volume of the business that follows this pattern in Africa's international trade, they cannot be expected to see the urgency of addressing this problem or, for that matter, the dangers of acceding to existing international copyright conventions or promulgating their local copyright laws based on existing international modules. The original intention of the Harare *Indaba* was to promote intra-African trade horizontally, so that African countries can be encouraged to trade with each other, not only in finished books but in rights as well, so that an African market in books can be engendered and strengthened. You cannot eat your cake and still have it. By going about this noble objective in the way that it did, the *Indaba* squandered a rare opportunity. It would have been more meaningful if African publishers had talked among themselves first and formed a pressure group to plead with foreign publishers to adopt a humane approach in their copyright administration policies, than to sit with them at the same table and be taught how to deal in rights—as if that was the only problem.

The international watchdog agencies that police copyright infringement are not geared towards protecting copyright in works originating from Africa. They are concerned more with guarding the interests of the North whose publishers produce the majority of copyrightable materials. African publishers themselves, with or without assistance from their own governments, do not have the capacity, know-how, experience or even the will to defend the little that they have. At the Harare conference, stories were told of foreign publishers who publish the works of African scholars without even notifying them or signing any form of agreement. A sharp exchange arose between one foreign agent who was busy negotiating rights with the estate of a dead writer whose book was, in fact, still in print with Tanzania Publishing House! We are ourselves aware that publishers in Germany, Italy, Japan, etc., continue to publish certain titles originally published by the now defunct East African Publishing House (EAPH) even though that company has been long bankrupt, and some of the authors have transferred their rights to other local rights holders. Attempts to get those publishers to confirm or deny this have fallen on deaf ears, even when we have sought the assistance of their embassies in Nairobi. In some cases, we have been informed that the books have gone out of print, yet one sometimes spots copies of these licensed editions, usually in translation, on display at such fairs as Frankfurt and Bologna.

My company has dealt in the rights trade perhaps more than any other African publisher outside South Africa. We have nearly 100 licensed titles on our list, approximately 15% of our backlist and have had rights dealings in at least 50 of our locally originated titles. We have been subjected to some of the prejudices mentioned above, although we must admit that we have found

American publishers more understanding and more sympathetic to our requests than their British counterparts, especially in their readiness to grant rights faster and on better terms. Admittedly, we have not dealt with the Americans on licensing their textbooks, as our business, to date, has been restricted mainly to African studies publications. The majority of licenses grant us the Kenya market only, but in a few exceptional cases we get Kenya, Uganda and Tanzania, and sometimes even Africa. Only with James Currey Publishers[12] in London do we have co-publication arrangements which enable each party to exploit the rights and market potential of each title to the full.

Humanizing International Copyright

Africa's publishing capacity is bound to increase in future, thanks to the interest that African governments, international donor agencies and non-governmental organizations are beginning to show in this sector. The activities of the African Publishers Network, (APNET), formed two years ago, are drawing sympathetic and active support even from NGO's and donor agencies in the North—including the World Bank, which has become a major player on the African book publishing scene. The Bank is currently revising its book procurement procedures with a view to encouraging more books and materials acquisition through Local Competitive Bidding (LCB) and direct contracting more than the International Competitive Bidding (ICB) approach it has used in the past, and which has tended to favor foreign suppliers and suppress local participation in the tendering process. Others are assisting in training, capitalizing, and strengthening the marketing and distribution structures, as well as encouraging the growth of local and regional publishers' associations, and of course giving support to the APNET itself.

At the same time, African governments are beginning to appreciate the need to liberalize and privatize the industry, delink it from the state, and generally create an even playing field where quality and fair competition will be the hallmark. These efforts are likely to result in a more invigorated African publishing industry in the next decade or two, but they are unlikely to stem the negative impact of international copyright, now or then, unless attention is given to the recommendations which follow. We shall make these as simply, clearly, and as tentatively as possible and on the premises that, while fulfilling the original intentions of international copyright, they will help to facilitate maximum exploitation of the world's intellectual property to benefit all. The overriding assumptions behind the proposals, as explained above, include the need to develop and expand publishing capacity in the developing world through maximizing the transfer of knowledge from the rich to the book poor countries. It is also assumed that a need exists to standardize the rules, written or unwritten, that currently guide collective copyright administration by rights holders as enforced by their national, regional and international copyright monitoring agencies and reinforced by their governments. Finally, it is assumed that the collective administration of copyright should, first and foremost, be in the interest of knowledge, rather than for the advancement of trade, although we recognize the rights of writers and other creators to be rewarded for their creations. We shall first deal with what should or can be done now and conclude by making some suggestions for the future.

Authors' contracts are drawn by publishers in the North for their own authors and for those who seek reprint licenses from them. These contracts should be examined again and again to continually determine to what extent they conform to the letter and spirit of international copyright and national copyright laws. The rules governing their granting of licenses, or their refusal to grant such licenses, must be subjected to international scrutiny with a view to having them revised to incorporate the human factor, and all publishers should be prevented from directly refusing to grant reprint licenses on flimsy grounds or without giving reasons.

International copyright agencies such as WIPO, International Publishers Copyright Council (IPCC), Copyright Clearance Center (CCC) in the United States, Copyright Licensing Agency (CLA) in the U.K., and other national Reproduction Rights Organizations (RROs), working closely with publishers and governments of the developed world should provide a two-way service in their copyright protection activities. As we have pointed out in this essay, publishers in the North continue to flout with impunity the same conventions that are protecting their interests in the South. As a demonstration of transparency and good faith, these agencies should recruit more Africans into their organizations to help tilt their policies and focus towards the developing world. Further, they or any others affiliated to them should devise a mechanism for releasing, on a regular basis, a list of out-print-titles with tips on which major titles are about to go out of print, and which ones are back in print. These lists should be widely publicized, especially in the South so that any publishers wishing to re-issue some of these titles may make the necessary arrangements to do so. Finally, the foreign publishers who insist on being granted world rights by the African writers they contract and who then sell some of those rights to the United States or other rights buyers on the writers' behalf must do this with the full knowledge and consent of the writers. In most cases, the African writer has little knowledge and no control over such a sale, or any sale of subsidiary rights for that matter, so that when a book thus sold goes out of print in those subsidiary markets, the rights revert to the foreign publisher rather than to the author who is the rightful owner, and to add insult to injury information about such transaction is not always conveyed to the writer, unless he makes a specific request for it. Presently, these international rights agencies are putting far too much emphasis on matters of piracy and copyright infringement and although these are important, international copyright should be seen as playing a positive and broadening role, rather than appear all the time to be limiting the frontiers of knowledge distribution.

We have pointed out elsewhere in this essay that many publishers in the South are not familiar with the finer points of international copyright and its collective administration. Although we are aware that some attempts have been made and are being made to increase the quantity and quality of information related to copyright and its use as well as its abuse this information is not being made available throughout the world and at all levels. Current efforts appear to be directed mainly at governments, and we would advise that public, private, international and other specialized publishing institutions and professional associations be included, placed on the mailing list of these agencies and be considered for the training that is offered from time to time. The broader issues of equity and copyright control and collective bargaining and management should form part of the training awareness package offered at such courses.

The rules governing compulsory acquisition remain vague and are misunderstood by many. The majority of African publishers are ignorant of them. We are aware that there are certain provisions, brokered by UNESCO, which permit compulsory acquisition in cases where rights holders refuse to grant or unreasonably withhold copyright. Be this as it may, we are not, to this day, aware of any African publisher who has acquired rights in this way. The reasons for this include lack of capacity referred to above, and the fact that African publishers have little knowledge about how to go about this process and which titles, if any, are available for such acquisition. Many African publishers would like to acquire rights to the writings of their first generation creative writers whose copyrights are held by publishers in the North. Often their requests are rejected outright or frustrated and delayed for reasons which can only be described as selfish and opportunistic. In some cases, these books might be prescribed as set books for schools, and thousands of copies may be required. Due to the scarcity of foreign exchange and unaffordable prices, African countries are not always in a position to buy these books abroad. It would be more meaningful for the foreign publisher to sub-license such books to a local publisher who might be able to make copies more readily available at an affordable price. It is obvious that the original publisher cannot sell such a book in as many numbers as the local publisher could. One British publisher once told the writer that he was not ready to part with his "birthright" when requested for a sub-license on a title by one of his African authors for sale in the East African market.

The works of Shakespeare, Dickens, Jane Austen, Tolstoy, Chekhov, Gogol, Ibsen, Brecht, Kafka, Goethe, to name only a few, are very popular in Africa and are constantly prescribed for study in schools. African publishers have experienced problems in securing rights to these books in almost all cases. How come that the works of these long dead literary geniuses are not yet in the public domain? What should African publishers do to gain access to them? But, then, if they cannot even secure rights to the works of their own writers, what chances do they have of obtaining rights to long-established classics? This clearly is an area where a lot more work remains to be done by the purveyors of international copyright, especially KOPINOR of Norway, who are currently spending large sums of money in defense of rights holders in the United States still fighting for their "full" rights[13].

A meaningful future strategy would call for formulation of policies at national, regional and international levels, supported by financial and technical assistance from IFRRO, RRO's, national governments, NGO's, the World Bank and other aid agencies in the North, to strengthen African publishing industries and delink them from state control and management. Pressing issues such as lack of capital, technical and management skills, and capacity to effectively distribute their products within their own borders and for export should be tackled if an industry capable of fulfilling the educational needs of its country and the continent as a whole is to emerge. In other words, African publishers should be enabled to expand their capacity through full participation in the prime and relatively risk-free educational markets so that they can muster the resources to begin to devote attention to other publishing areas such as fiction, children's books, academic books, biographies and other general and trade books which are easier to export to other markets or likely to be candidates for rights dealings. Gradually they will begin to appreciate the need to protect their intellectual property and their membership to these international copyright conventions will begin to make sense. Although such compensation would still not be adequate, at least it would go some way in correcting the present unbalanced state of affairs.

Future research projects should be initiated on a joint basis, teaming up local and international scholars and should be guided by limited copyright protocols[14]. The findings should then be published locally or jointly with international publishers and the copyright in those works should rest with local publishers who should originate the head contracts. There is another example in the kind of arrangements presently in force between the enterprising British publisher James Currey and several African publishers. Each party takes the market territory they think they can effectively cover and the rest is left open for whoever gets there first. In this way, the African publisher is able not only to gain exposure outside his home market, but also garners experience in the complicated world of international copyright trading.

Thirdly, since African countries are still largely oral societies, we would urge that oral literatures and traditions be exempted from international copyright and national copyright laws in Africa. No scholar or researcher should be allowed to claim copyright on materials collected freely from rural folk, or even when certain token payments have been made for this information or such copyrights should be limited by both national laws and international copyright conventions as suggested above. In this way, we shall be forestalling the prospect of having to seek to reclaim these copyrights from foreign researchers and their publishers in the North at a future date. And while on the issue of reclaiming copyright, we would propose that an attempt be made by African governments, publishers, and their authors to reclaim copyrights in works, especially fiction, originally published outside the continent but which are now urgently required for educational purposes. Attempts to obtain sub-licenses by individual publishers for certain markets have to date been less than successful.

Fourthly, African copyright laws should make it mandatory for a foreign publisher who acquires rights from an African publisher to make a full acknowledgment of this fact in his own edition. The practice will not only expose and promote the African publisher to the international market but will also al-firm that he is the holder of the copyright contained in the work.

Fifthly, African governments should monitor and, if found necessary, license specialized foreign book agents who come to Africa to buy rare books, including out-of-print titles and gray literature, as some of these publications may not be copyrighted, and there could be a danger that the copyrights in these books could be exported purely by the very act of buying all the copies available in Africa.

Sixthly, aware of the imbalance in the flow of copyright reproduction fees, but anxious that publishers in the South should operate within the international copyright system, some IFRRO member organizations have agreed that copyright fees collected through national RRO's should, at least for the first few years, remain in that country to support publishing activities there. This is a welcome compensating message of goodwill and noble intention and should be adopted by all the national RR's currently in operation worldwide, and their 37 associate members. It is only by seeing the fruits of copyright protection that African publishers can develop confidence in the collective administration of international copyright and appreciate that it potentially stands to benefit them and that the motives of international rights holders are honorable and responsive to their welfare.

Finally, a word about the English language. English has spread to become a truly international language. Not only have the traditional English-speaking countries like the United States, Britain, and India, grown in importance among the world's major book producers, non-English-speaking countries such as Germany, the Netherlands, Sweden, Norway and, to a smaller extent Japan, have increased their publishing output in that language. Most of the new research being carried out worldwide is done and disseminated, to a very large extent, in English. In Africa, most states have chosen English (or French) as their official language, in preference to their own languages, and have adopted it as the language of instruction in most cases after the first two or three years of primary education. The other foreign languages prevalent in Africa, namely French, Portuguese, and Afrikaans have also suffered at the expense of English, South Africa and Namibia being the latest countries to adopt it as their official language and Mozambique reportedly considering adopting it. These new realities make it necessary for international copyright conventions to adopt a softer stance to requests for same-language reprint rights in the same way as previous conventions had simplified access to translation rights. Our view here is that with the growing dominance of English as a world language, same-language English reprint rights are becoming increasingly more important than translation rights.

These are only a few of the remedial measures that can be taken to stem the flight of African copyrights while functioning within the provision of international copyright. A more permanent solution would be to subject the provisions themselves to scrutiny and to amend those sections which are inimical to the needs of the developing world. These would include considering a reduction in the duration of copyright, strengthening the clauses dealing with education exemption, compulsory acquisition, fair dealing, simplifying the assignment of copyright clauses, and providing more effective guidelines in the treatment of oral literatures and traditions, to mention only a few.

Conclusion

In this essay, we have not sought to explain or interpret the various laws and protocols governing international copyright, although we are familiar with them. Rather, we have attempted, in simple and accessible language, to highlight the inherent dangers and weaknesses contained in those conventions, both in their letter and practice. We have observed that African states are faced with a choice of two evils—to sign or not to sign. They have little or nothing to benefit from signing, and little or nothing to lose by not signing. We have found no evidence of advantages or disadvantages either way, although it can be argued that by signing, book poor African countries have compromised their human right of access to knowledge, and they will realize their folly when they will have acquired the much-needed capacity to exploit these works, only to discover that the protectionism inherent in these conventions and sealed by their own signatures have prohibit them from doing so.

We would not advocate that African states, or the developing world for that matter, should close their borders to the outside world, as was done by some of now developed countries, until they have achieved a level of development that can enable them to meaningfully participate in the present international copyright order, attractive though such a proposal might sound. Instead we have advocated for equity, honesty, reciprocity, understanding and fair play so that the African signatories can be compensated for the bold, courageous and selfless step they have taken in recognition of the noble aims of international copyright conventions.

The North must realize that its continued prosperity depends to a certain extent on the developing world, Africa included, and may even be at the expense of it. There is a limit to the extent to which such dependency relationship can be sustained, now that increasing poverty in the South is already making it impossible for meaningful trade between the two blocs to take place. It is with this in mind that we have proposed that the North should accept a measure of responsibility in correcting the present imbalances, and should initiate and/or support programs (some of which have been suggested here) to strengthen the economies of African states and their publishing industries—in particular by playing a leading role in humanizing international copyright so that it may serve the needs of knowledge dissemination more effectively and for the benefit of all.

Notes

1 An Ndebele word which means "meeting" usually called to reconcile groups or sort out differences.

2 The majority of readers find the book difficult and slow to read and does not offer much entertainment value compared to other knowledge distribution technologies.

3 This information is contained in the working paper of a WIPO Regional Seminar on Copyright and Neighboring Rights for African Countries, held in Nairobi in July 1994.

4 For more details, see bibliography.

5 Ibid., note 3 above.

6 For more details, see bibliography.

7 See paper by Eamon T. Fennessy in *Logos,*. 4, (No. 3, 1993).

8 Chapter 1 of his *Book Publishing in a Societal Context: Japan and the West,* see bibliography.

9 This was a copyright case between Evans Brothers (UK) and Heinemann Kenya Ltd., (presently known as East African Educational Publishers Ltd.) over a local edition, published by the latter, of Mohammed Said Abdalla's Kiswahili novel *Kisima cha Giningi.*

10 Kiswahili is a Kenya language spoken by most peoples of East and Central Africa.

11 Mr. Justice Frank Shields, formerly Judge, High Court of Kenya.

12 Their full address is: James Currey Publishers., 54b Thomhill Square, Islington, London. NI IBE, U. K.

13 This information was made available to the writer by John-Willy Rudolph, Executive Director of KOPINOR, Norway, during a recent visit to that country.

14 *Ibid.,* this provision in international copyright was also explained to the writer by KOPINOR.

Bibliography

African Rights *Indaba* 1994—Conference Papers [currently in draft - to be published by Zimbabwe International Book Fair 1995].

Altbach, Philip G., *The Knowledge Context: Comparative Perspectives on the Distribution of Knowledge* (Albany: State University of New York Press, 1987).

Altbach, Philip G., ed., *Publishing and Development in the Third World* (Oxford: Hans Zell Publishers, 1992).

Altbach, Philip G., ed., *Readings on Publishing in Africa and the Third World* (Buffalo, N.Y.: Bellagio Publishing Network, 1993).

Altbach, Philip G., Amadio A. Arboleda and S. Gopinathan, eds., *Publishing in the Third World: Knowledge and Development* (Portsmouth, N. H.: Heinemann, 1985).

Clark, Charles *Publishing Agreements: A Book of Precedents,* 4th edition, (London: Allen and Unwin, 1993).

Fennessy, Eamon T., "US Copyright Expert Goes to Nigeria and is Impressed," *Logos* 4 (No. 3, 1993)

Flint, Michael F., A *User's Guide to Copyright,* 3rd edition (London: Butterworths, 1990)

Gopinathan, S., ed., *Academic Publishing in ASEAN: Problems and Prospects* (Singapore: Festival of Books, 1986).

Graham, Gordon, *As I was Saying* (Oxford: Hans Zell, 1993).

Gunderson, Hakon and John-Willy Rudolph. *Together As One, Seminar on Copyright and Collective Administration of Rights Within the SADCC* (Oslo, Norway: KOPINOR, 1992)

Minowa, Shigeo *Book Publishing in a Societal Context: Japan and the West* (Tokyo: Japan Scientific Societies Press, 1990).

The Kenya Copyright Act, Cap. 130, Laws of Kenya (Nairobi: Government Printer, revised edition, 1991). [This laws is currently being amended.]

UNESCO, *Statistical Year Book* 1993 (Paris: UNESCO, 1993).

Chapter 3

COPYRIGHT:
A PERSPECTIVE FROM THE DEVELOPING WORLD

Dina Nath Malhotra

The last four decades of the Twentieth century have witnessed a global explosion of information, with a large part of the colonial world becoming independent of the rule of European nations. One of many results of this information explosion has been increased concern over the concept of copyright and the various problems connected with it. Copyright, which used to be an issue of concern only to the developed world, has become the concern of all the civilized nations engaged in the spread of information and education. For reasons both of economic interest as well as the desire to protect intellectual creativity on the part of the developed world, vigorous action has been initiated in the copyright field internationally.

Now, whatever is happening to the copyright laws in the countries of Asia or for that matter in Africa or Latin America, has become the concern of European nations. The issues are not as simple as they seem. The newly emerging nations of Asia and Africa have come to understand that for the advancement of their countries, they must make a substantial scholarly contribution to the field of education and learning. They have realized that the quality of human material has to be improved so that their citizens can work and compete for the progress of their country with the citizens of the advanced countries.

Education and information are key areas in which every nation wants to improve. On the other hand, advanced nations are not often concerned about the progress of developing countries except when their own economic interests are affected. It is for the benefit of their own citizens that European nations work for the protection of copyright internationally. What the countries of the Berne Union had done in 1886 to safeguard their interests among the European nations, motivates them today to look after their economic interests all over the world wherever their books and other forms of intellectual property are marketed. Concern for the protection of (and encouragement for) intellectual creativity may be advocated in the name of the author, yet the basic motivation is the protection of the economic interests of their own country and citizens.

The question of intellectual property which was previously discussed only by WIPO or UNESCO has been brought in the orbit of GATT. Previously, books and other educational and entertainment materials were small in quantity and mostly confined to their respective countries of origin. Now, these are traveling beyond national borders and reaching all corners of the world without any time lag. Forty years ago, international copyright agreements were understood by only a few experts in the field. Today, these are being discussed by people on a wide spectrum, even though they may not understand the subject in its various aspects.

Lack of Awareness of the Concept of Copyright

Unfortunately, the concept of copyright has not been understood by many in developing countries. The concept that writing is the property of the author or the intellectual, and that his property needs to be protected like other material property, is not quite realized. There has not been any tradition in the developing countries of an author writing for money or remuneration. It has been taken for granted that any wise man writing something is motivated by the ideal of doing good to the society. The idea of financial remuneration to the writer of the book was alien to ancient societies. This explains the genesis of the basic problem of the lack of understanding of the concept of copyright in developing societies. Ancient societies worked on the assumption that the worldly needs of the sages, the wise men, the intellectuals and the writers were to be taken care of by the society. Therefore, the idea of payment to the writer, and that the writings of an author were his property, seemed quite naive to them.

This point has to be explained at length, in order to clarify why the concept of copyright is not understood in developing countries. Naturally, this situation leads to some problems. In order to counteract these, we have to create a climate in which there is an appreciation for the concept of copyright, and its significance is properly understood. The public has to be educated and informed that copyright in writings, paintings, music compositions, etc., is as much a property as a house and a building. Unauthorized use of these creations by others amounts to stealing, just as of property or a commodity. Basically, people have to understand that just as a person builds a house or buys a commodity, similarly an intellectual by writing a book creates a property. The intellectual has as much right to enjoy, and the right to protection of the fruits of his labor from writing a book as a property owner has.

I may relate a case here which was very surprising for me. I observed the attitude of a journalist in a developing country who could not understand why the pirated editions of foreign books available on the pavements were a legal as well as a moral crime against the writer of the original book, and was like a case of stealing someone else's property. He was happy that costly foreign books were available on the pavements at cheaper prices for the benefit of the public. It took me some time to explain to him how one would feel if one's jacket is stolen and sold in the market to someone else at a cheaper price. Stolen goods are always cheaper, but can we justify stealing because it makes available commodities cheaper to the public at large? In essence, we must explain to the public that copyright is as much a property and needs to be protected and enjoyed as any other property.

If we look at the situation in developing countries with this background, we have to realize that when an unauthorized use of copyright material is made in a developing country, it is by and large due to a lack of understanding of the concept of copyright, rather than by any desire on the part of the user to deprive another person of his rightful gain. Sometimes even editors and publishers are unaware of the laws of copyright, not to speak of the general public.

So, there is a fundamental need to disseminate knowledge about the concept and use of copyright material in developing countries. This should be done by the governments, associations of authors and publishers, copyright boards and intellectuals, through organizing seminars and training courses, as well as publishing manuals and literature on this subject. At the international level, WIPO has been doing very useful work by imparting training in copyright to representatives of developing countries. These courses have been well-organized and designed and the Copyright Division for Developing Countries deserves much appreciation for this. My suggestion in this regard is that we should ensure that those who benefit by these training courses should be charged with the responsibility to organize further training courses in copyright when they return to their respective countries.

Publishers' associations have a special role to play in this respect as it is the publisher who, in actual practice, serves as a custodian of the rights of the authors. In India, the Federation of Indian Publishers attaches special importance to the propagation and protection of copyright in the interests of the publishers and the authors. There is a very strong "Working Group on Copyright," now a "Copyright Council" which organizes training courses in copyright and has plans to issue manuals on copyright in the current year's program.

Copyright and Development

The needs and interests of the developing countries may be different from those of the advanced countries. But, in order to have a meaningful world-wide understanding and protection of copyright, there has to be a common ground where the two can meet.

India became independent in 1947, and many other countries became free within the following decade. India, along with other countries, realized the need of educating its citizens and providing them with reading materials. Their most urgent requirement was the rapid transfer of knowledge, particularly in the fields of science and technology from the industrially advanced countries to meet their educational needs. In such a transfer, the role of books is crucial. How to get them? A large scale import of foreign books was no solution. On the other hand, if the developing countries were to resort to unauthorized reproduction/translation of books of foreign origin, it would create an unhealthy situation.

In this context, the whole question of the justice and validity of International Copyright Conventions became a matter of debate and questioning. There were some in India who advocated that the Indian Government should free itself from the shackles of the Copyright Conventions and publish freely all books needed for the education of its students. Their argument was that if the Soviet

Union did not bother about the international copyright, why could not India do the same? If the United States could remain out of the international conventions until 1952 and publish all the required books, why should India retard her progress by these conventions? Let India have a holiday in copyright for a decade or so, publish all the books needed for its students and then consider re-entering the circle of international copyright conventions.

But India, with its commitment to the copyright system and especially under its first Prime Minister Jawahar Lal Nehru, decided to examine the possibility as to whether these conventions could be amended suitably so that adherence to these conventions did not come in the way of providing books for the education of students in developing countries. Any international convention endures in practice if it can satisfy reasonably the aspirations of all concerned. It cannot be sustained on the basis of the interests of some nations and to the detriment of others. Sooner or later such conventions fail, or even if these continue, they exist on paper, but in practice would not be followed. After all, 'enlightened self-interest' is the basic guideline for countries when they discuss international agreements. High principles may be propounded, great moral debates may be held—but at the base of these is the self-interest of the countries concerned.

So the question arose of amending the international copyright treaties. The European countries, to start with, looked askance at the suggestions of developing countries for change in the copyright norms in international conventions. It seemed strange to them that developing countries—which until yesterday were their colonies—could dare to raise such blasphemous issues which affected the sanctity of copyright. A great deal of negotiation took place, culminating in 1967 in crystallizing the aspirations of developing countries into the 'Stockholm Protocol.'

It was not an easy task. There was a lot of give and take. The representatives of the advanced countries had heard about the rumblings in developing countries and demand for complete exit from copyright conventions by those countries. So they understood that unless something was done, the whole superstructure could fall apart. It was an act of wisdom on the part of the leaders of both the developed and developing countries, to devise a solution—albeit a compromise formula with many provisions and clauses. Anyway, the tide for abrogation of international copyright conventions was stemmed by this act. Unfortunately, some of the leading countries which had agreed to sign the Stockholm Protocol went back on their word and again there was an impasse. However, the determination of saner elements on both sides led to the final approval of the Paris Act in 1971.

The Paris Act

It was a great achievement, though it did not satisfy the needs of developing countries. The provision of 'compulsory licensing' was made a way out wherein recalcitrant copyright holders in advanced countries could be forced to part with their copyrights in favor of a developing country when it was urgently needed for the purpose of education, research, etc. Though apparently it was considered to be a gesture to fulfill the needs of developing countries, in actual practice it was made so impracticable, with so many difficult provisions that it turned out to be not worth pursuing. Yet, it had a great psychological and educative impact on the copyright holders of advanced countries, who realized that if they do not voluntarily give copyright licenses to publishers of developing countries on reasonable terms, there is provision for an infrastructure in both the copyright conventions by which their copyrights could be taken away against their will.

There are very few known cases where the provision of compulsory licensing has been resorted to by publishers of developing countries to take rights from unwilling copyright holders in advanced countries. But as I said, the effect has been beneficial and as I use the term 'Sword of Damocles' for the provision of 'compulsory licensing' which puts apprehension in the minds of copyright holders that if they do not accede to reasonable demands from the publishers of developing countries for giving them copyrights, these could be taken away under the new provisions.

Nobody has made a survey of the total scene and come to any statistically based inference that after passing of the Paris Act whether there has been any massive flow of copyrights from advanced countries to developing countries. It is true, of course, that things have changed and leading publishers in industrialized countries have set up their own branches in developing countries and published cheaper economy editions of their costly books so that, firstly, nobody can apply for compulsory licensing if the prices are at the national level and secondly, to expand their own base of publishing business abroad.

I believe that the leaders of developing countries did not have in their minds the economic interests of their publishing industry when they pressed for amendment of the international copyright conventions. Their aim clearly was to provide books for their reading public both in educational institutions as well as general readers at affordable prices. The idea was not to rob the economic interests of the publishers in the advanced world and give it over to the publishers in their own countries. But the clear aim was to make it possible for the readers of developing world to get books at prices which they can afford. Therefore, when the publishers of advanced countries brought out their economy editions for distribution in developing countries nobody could press for compulsory licensing for the benefit of the publishers of the developing countries. It has been provided in the conditions of compulsory licensing that if the publishers of the advanced countries themselves make available their books at cheaper prices for the benefit of the students in developing countries then the provisions of compulsory licensing cannot be invoked.

In the context of the publishing interests of advanced countries, it was more a business and economic consideration, rather than their love for the interest of the reading public of developing countries, which made them bring out economy editions.

Committee for Access to Copyright Materials
In order to stimulate the transfer of copyrights from advanced countries, a 'Joint Committee of UNESCO and WIPO For Getting Access to Copyright Materials to Developing Countries' was established. The aim of this exercise was, after incorporating provisions of the Paris Act in both the Berne Convention and the Universal Copyright Convention, to provide some actual flow of rights to developing countries. Whatever difficulties came in the way should be examined by this Joint Committee and steps taken so that the intention of the Paris Act was achieved. The objectives in the formation of this Committee were very good but unfortunately in actual practice, it could not achieve anything worthwhile. I

speak from experience as I was the first Chairman of this committee. Firstly, the committee met only once a year, and later on meetings were canceled because the funds were not available for bringing the members to the venue of the committee meetings.

Then, even in the first meeting, an unrealistic approach was made in propagating the notion that all publishers of advanced countries should provide lists of books whose copyrights could be given to publishers from the developing countries. This very basic decision was wrong and impractical. The Paris Act was passed to get copyrights for those books which were not being parted with and not for those which were being willingly given by copyright owners. Long range programs were chalked out to be implemented in a couple of years, but in time people forgot about these.

As the Chairman of the committee, I requested that instructions be given to the secretariat at UNESCO to give at least quarterly reports regarding the progress made in that direction. It was said to be an impossible task. It became quite clear that this was a wishy-washy affair just to show that something was being done. I am sorry to say that nothing was achieved out of this committee and it soon disappeared.

The question that arose in the minds of people was whether or not copyright holders in advanced countries had felt a change of heart and wanted really to part with the copyrights of the works which were urgently needed in developing countries for education. The passage of the Paris Act was one thing, but implementation had a different story to tell. Looking at the whole situation, my view is that even though the compulsory licensing procedure has not worked, the psychological effect of pinpointing the needs of developing countries has been good.

Subsidy for Publishing

The governments of some advanced countries established programs that subsidized their publishers to make available cheaper editions of their books for marketing in developing countries where the high-priced original editions could not be sold. In this respect, the cases of two governments are well known. The U.S. government made funds available to the publishers in developing countries for bringing out cheaper editions on the one hand and on the other they gave benefit to the copyright holders in the U.S. by giving them royalty on the basis of their original American prices for the copyrighted books given for publication in developing countries. This was a very wise scheme which encouraged U.S. publishers to give rights and also made available cheaper books in developing countries so that these could compete with the local books. These books were well written by experts but not tailored to the needs of developing countries. Yet being good books, they made a dent into the market.

On the other hand, the government of the United Kingdom gave funds to British publishers for producing cheaper editions of books published in the UK, to be exported to developing countries with the objective of keeping British books in the market and not letting them be ousted due to their high prices. In this case, the publishers of developing countries could not participate and it worked only for the benefit of the British publishers. Both the US and UK governments had the interests of their own publishing industries at heart and helped them to remain in the market in the face of competition from the domestic publishing industries in developing countries.

The question, as to how much these economy editions benefited the students and the reading public of developing countries, was hotly debated by experts. Some people argued that these better quality books at cheaper prices gave unfair competition to the publishers in developing countries. Local publishers on the strength of their own funds without subsidy from anyone could not produce matching books. It has been said that foreign books will oust local books to the detriment of the domestic authors and publishers. Further, such an outcome would harm national authorship and depress the local publishing industry. It was considered to be a case of 'dumping' foreign goods in order to kill the local industry. Of course, every book is a different entity and cannot be a substitute for others. Yet, in general terms, it was a case of 'dumping' by stronger foreign industries to kill the local growing industry.

In the case of India, where this question was hotly debated, the Government of India provided funds to the National Book Trust of India for starting a subsidy scheme for Indian Publishers to bring out cheaper editions of their text books so that they could compete with the imported British and American Books. However, this program was on a small scale, though a laudable one.

Viewpoint of the Developed Countries

Let us examine the psyche of the publishers in advanced countries who hold most of the copyright material needed for education in the disciplines of science and technology. These publishers naturally want to sell their own books, even though very highly priced, in developing countries. This is obviously more appealing to them than giving a license to a publisher of a developing country to bring out a reprint. Of course, in giving the translation rights, they have a more positive approach because that does not cut into their business and gives them something additional which they cannot themselves earn.

The attitude of the average copyright-holder in advanced countries a kind of 'dog in the manger' policy. The publisher would prefer to neither make the book available at affordable prices in a developing country, nor give license to a publisher in a developing country to bring out a cheaper edition. The argument is that the publisher makes more money on fewer of his own high priced books exported to a developing country than by giving copyright license. They calculate that they will get even much less from a large number of cheaper edition published by a local publisher because royalties will be on the basis of the price of the cheaper edition. So far as narrow personal economic interest is concerned, he is right to hold such views. However, the publisher forgets that by giving the rights for a cheaper edition, net earnings or royalties may initially be low, but ultimately if books sell in larger numbers (the result of the local publisher gaining the rights), the original publisher will earn much more. Then, there will be a chance for many other books of this publishing house to be sold in the developing country in collaboration with the local publisher.

Secondly, the publisher is apprehensive over whether there will be adequate royalties, on time and according to the agreement signed. There are some cases where the publisher of a developing country may not have remitted the royalty on time. There are also cases in which royalties were not honestly or accurately calculated. But these are stray cases of black sheep which occur everywhere. Another reason before the copyright-holder to worry is that when the royalty is being remitted from a developing country, two obstacles come in the way. The first is that due to the paucity of foreign exchange in some countries, as well as very laborious formalities, royalties take a lot of time to reach their intended recipients. Furthermore, sometimes the taxes imposed on royalties to be remitted are quite high. Therefore, the net amount which reaches the copyright holders of the advanced countries ultimately becomes meager, delayed and not worth their negotiating an agreement.

Now, it is for the publishers and the governments of developing countries to sort out these problems, among others which hinder the efficient remittance of royalties to the copyright-holders in advanced countries. Some of the countries have entered into treaties for avoidance of double taxation so that the tax deducted at the source in the remitting country does not put the receiver at a disadvantage. The copyright holder in the advanced countries can use that receipt to get a deduction in tax from the Revenue Department of his own country without cost to him.

I have advocated that there should be no tax on royalties at all. Unfortunately, the word 'royalty' connotes something royal. The royalties in cases of industrial licensing, which are in astronomical figures, may be taxed, but the 'copyright fees' called 'royalties' should not be taxed at all. This has been my plea to the governments of developing countries. In order to encourage the copyright-holders in advanced countries to give licenses to publishers of developing countries there are certain things which must be done by the governments and publishers of the developing countries.

I firmly believe that the governments of developing countries will ultimately not be losers in their revenue receipts by making the royalties to be remitted abroad completely free from tax. If the governments of developing countries took this action, there would be greater flow of copyrights into developing countries and the national publishing industry would flourish much more. With this expansion of business and prosperity in the national publishing industry, the governments will be able to net more revenue on the business taxation of the local publishers. This may seem imperceptible today, but ultimately it will be a gain for the respective country, as local publishers flourish while the government's revenues do not become less in the final tally.

There is one more problem in this context which should be stated. The copyright-holders of advanced countries give license to publish within a particular territory of a developing country. But the publishers of developing countries do not honor thoroughly the terms of the agreements and sometimes allow export of their indigenous cheaper editions to other countries knowingly or unknowingly. This upsets the market of the copyright holders of advanced countries and they feel cheated. If the game is to be played fairly, the publishers and their associates should guarantee that such actions as the unauthorized export of books to other countries will not take place. Of course, a few copies can trickle without the knowledge of the local publisher through some jobbers, but this should not be mistaken for a willful default of responsibility.

Understanding Needed

What emerges from these problems is that there should be a relationship of complete understanding and sincere dealing on the part of the publishers on all sides. It is through understanding the interests of the parties concerned that a rational and lasting solution can be sorted out. This can come through greater communication between the publishers of all countries. The International Publishers Association, in its seminars and conferences, brings together publishers of both the developing and developed world. Similarly, the Frankfurt Book Fair and other international book fairs provide an opportunity where publishers from all over the world rub shoulders with one another. By more personal meetings and with a conscious effort to appreciate interests of the other parties, many tangles can be solved.

The role played by leading publishers who understand international copyright problems is of great value. There are cases when copyright holders in advanced countries asked for impossible terms because they did not know the prevailing conditions of publishing in developing countries, and some times they are not very interested in giving the copyright material on a reasonable basis because it does not bring much money to them.

I remember one case in which an educational publisher from India wrote for permission to include two poems in a selection from a British publisher. In spite of reminders, the Indian publisher did not get any reply. He was to submit that book for approval as a text book in one of the states of India, and finally without waiting for the permission, he included those poems in his book, hoping that if the book were approved he would follow up the matter with the British publisher and get the permission. When the book was approved as a text book, the Indian publisher wrote to the British publisher for permission, explaining that the book had been approved, and he must get the required consent of the copyright holder. The British publisher, in this case, without knowing the grounded realities nor the total sale price or quantity of the book, asked for £500 for the inclusion of those two poems.

The Indian publisher was in a fix and in a delicate position, not knowing what to do, and brought the case to me. I checked up as to how large a portion those two poems were of the total book, the total expected sale of the book and price of the book. Having collected accurate data, I came to the conclusion that this was a small slow-selling optional book, and £25 were more than enough. I wrote about this matter to a leading British publisher who understood the situation in developing countries and believed in cordial relations. Fortunately, that British publisher, knowing my credentials, discussed the matter with the copyright holder and within a fortnight sent back the permission for exactly £25. Now, this case amply demonstrated that given good-will and understanding, it is possible to sort out many copyright cases. Certainly, the part played by personal contacts and participation in meetings is very important in international affairs, or may I say in all affairs of human relations. Harboring mutual suspicions and taking up impossible stands create serious problems.

Authors anywhere in the world always want their works to be published in as many countries as possible. Most are happier with the lower rate of royalty from a low-priced book sold in a developing country, than by not allowing his work to be published there at all, or restricted to the export of a few high-priced copies. There has been a clash of interests between authors and copyright holders in advanced countries. Many times authors have been annoyed that the copyright-holding publishers come in the way of wider dissemination of their books, solely because of their narrow economic interests. It is true that in today's world authors also want greater remuneration. But there have been cases on record, and there must be many more, wherein authors voluntarily and happily want to give the copyright of their works to publishers in developing countries, at lesser rates of royalty on reduced prices in those countries.

The other question which I want to raise in the context of international dissemination of protected works is about the term of copyright. Intellectual property rights, as we all know, is not a perennial right. It expires and falls into 'public domain' in various countries after the death of the author from a period of 25 years to, in extreme cases, 80 years. But it does fall into 'public domain' wherein anybody is free to publish that work without any payment to anyone and without any permission from anyone. There is only one perennial right in the copyright field—the moral right which means that the work cannot be distorted. This right remains forever and anybody can invoke it as a matter of public concern. This is provided to keep the sanctity and purity of the work.

The basic questions which emerge from this discussion is how far and to what extent the protection of copyright is sacrosanct, and at what stage and under what circumstances it should be relaxed. The objective of copyright to protect the interest of the creator, that is both of the author and the publisher, is of paramount importance. Without encouraging and protecting creativity, no country can progress in the works of mind and forge ahead. There should be copyright protection, both nationally and internationally. The other question which needs to be discussed is how far and for how long copyright protection should be given— and at what stage copyrighted work should fall into public domain.

The delay in the dissemination of knowledge throughout the world is dangerous. The disparity between various nations in their thought and development leads to many problems including tension leading to wars. Just as the works of mind have to be protected and encouraged, at the same time rules have to be made by which copyright protection does not become an obstacle in the way of dissemination, but acts as an instrument for better diffusion of knowledge in the world.

Chapter 4

The Issues at Stake:
An Indian Perspective on Copyright

Urvashi Butalia

Copyright is a complex issue and its rights and wrongs have been the subject of considerable debate for many years. Indeed, of all the issues in publishing, this is perhaps one on which there has been the longest ongoing debate, and one, ironically, about which people within the profession still know very little. A quarter of a century ago the debate was relatively simpler, with fewer actors in the game, and less complicated questions to address. Today, the rapid growth of new technologies and their ability to transcend geographical and political boundaries, as well as the questions raised in international discussions about definitions and redefinitions of intellectual property have further complicated the debate.

As with most other issues, the question of copyright also looks different when examined from different perspectives. For a developing country—which is what India is said to be—there will necessarily be a different way of approaching this debate, than for a developed country. As realities on the ground change, so do the terms of the debate. It is my contention that this debate has for too long been hampered by rather questionable assumptions about notions of 'developed' and 'developing' countries. It is as if the former have reached some kind of static and desirable state from which there is nowhere further to go, while the latter are in a state of perpetual motion, almost, but never quite, there. Yet, the truth of the matter is that neither the so-called developed nor the so-called developing countries are static or homogenous. They change, indeed they develop. It is because this simple fact has been sidelined in the international debate on copyright, that some countries are continually cast into the role of 'offenders' while others adopt the high moral ground. I will argue in this essay that until there is a fundamental shift in perception on both 'sides' that recognizes that everyone has a stake in copyright, the discussion will not move forward in a constructive way. However, the basis of this discussion needs to be a recognition of the continually changing situation on the ground, and an understanding of what this means for agreements internationally.

In the last decade, for example, India has grown into becoming a significant producer and distributor of knowledge worldwide. In terms of economic definitions, it may continue to be numbered among developing nations, its status is nonetheless very different even from that of its neighbors, who also come under the same rubric. Thus, the notion of developed and developing countries, which governs the debate on copyright, is one that ignores such complexities and differences among countries. In this day and age, it simplifies the world into two blocs that seem to be perpetually pitted against each other, and it glosses over the fact that there may be points at which the interests of developed and developing countries can converge, and others at which they can differ.

Why has the issue of copyright been so charged and so difficult to debate? This question becomes particularly important in the present context when practically all countries in the world are signatory to one or other—and sometimes both—copyright conventions, and both internationally and nationally, are agreed on the importance of copyright protection. At the heart of this debate, it seems to me, lies a contradiction: on the one hand, there is an assumption that knowledge should have free flow across the world, that it should know no barriers. But knowledge cannot be transmitted in some pure form: it comes packaged as a product, with a price, with certain conditions on its sale, and that is where the problems begin. It is this contradiction that allows for the debate to be couched often in moral tones, while what is really being discussed is markets and money. Knowledge is also inextricably tied in with power, power with money and both of those with history. Thus, we know today that the production of knowledge in the world is largely concentrated in those countries which have economic and political power. Being major producers of knowledge, the 'developed' countries are fearful of its 'misuse' by their 'less developed' counterparts. Since the early seventies, the debate on copyright has been particularly concerned with these problems, and their complexity has only increased over time.

Until a few years ago, it was possible to contain this debate, so to speak, within the covers of a book or the sleeve of a record. Today, with floppy disks, databases, digital storage, on line information, etc., and different views on how intellectual property should be defined, and indeed who owns it, this is no longer possible. Nor is it possible to impose territorial boundaries—a subject that has always been a troubled one in the debate, but one which becomes even more so because of the nature of new technologies.

Where, in all this, do authors, publishers, or readers, stand? Too often, in the debate, the rights of publishers and readers are not central. If an author has the right to have his or her work protected, a reader, anywhere in the world, has the right to be able to read or at least have access to the work, provided he/she is willing to pay. Yet, because of territorial boundaries and unequal resources, this is not always possible. Equally, publishers have some rights to works in which they have invested. These have been some of the most troubled areas in the discussion on copyright: pirates, in particular, as well as those countries that have been reluctant to become signatory to international agreements, have often drawn on this difficult premise, that if a reader has a right to a particular book, then anyone has the right to reproduce that book for the reader, and ownership questions do not apply to knowledge.

In addition to the above, copyright has to do, both nationally and internationally, with that most material—and important—of things, money. While, in theory, publishers the world over may be agreed that the best base for a healthy and egalitarian copyright system is the development of local publishing all over the world, it is also true that until such time as such publishing does develop, countries which need books offer very lucrative markets to those which have books and the resources to produce them. Recently, in a discussion with a representative of the U.S. Publishers' Association, I raised the question of why the U.S., which half a century ago had not even been signatory to the copyright agreements and which only recently joined the Berne Convention, was today so concerned to project itself as one of copyright's foremost proponents. The response was both realistic and revealing:

that the U.S. had little else to export now, other than intellectual property. (Everything that was being produced in the U.S. could now be produced elsewhere, often more cheaply and, in the case of Japan, more efficiently as well.) Some further exploration pointed to the truth of this: at the International Publishers' Association Congress in Delhi in 1992, Michael Manson, a British publisher pointed out that:

> Copyright industries of which we are part are not economically marginal—25 billion dollars in 1985 in Britain, 2.9 per cent of the Gross National Product (GNP), greater than car manufacturing.... Similar studies exist for Australia, New Zealand, Canada, the Netherlands, Sweden and the latest in the United States in 1990, which estimates that copyright industries contribute 5.8 per cent of the U.S. GNP, employing almost 5 per cent of the U.S. workforce.[1]

In this essay, I would like to look at some of these questions from the perspective of India. Although copyright relates to various forms of intellectual production, I will here limit myself mainly to printed materials, largely books. I will examine, also, the existence of copyright nationally, within India, and India's position in the debate internationally. I hope, by so doing, to point out how, over time, India's own priorities have changed as its publishing industry has developed, how there is often a gap between what is argued internationally and what exists at the national level (and this is not in India alone), which makes it difficult for international agreements to be easily enforceable within different countries. Thus, what might, from the outside, seem to be a violation of an international agreement, can actually be something quite different when seen from within the country. With copyright being tied so much to legislation and litigation, I hope to be able to show how this means that the ground is often shifting, a circumstance which makes for both ambivalence and confusion, and further complicates the debate. Not only this, but with things changing so rapidly, the awareness of the issues involved in copyright is even less than it was before. My basic premise is that it is no longer possible, and if anything it is not even constructive, to locate the issue of copyright internationally within the cultural baggage of 'us' (First World or developed countries who supposedly have a wealth of literature to sell), and 'them' (Third

World or developing countries who have nothing of their own but are waiting to take, illegally, what the developed countries have to offer). Rather, it is important to look at the realities, both nationally and internationally, and to look at how best it is possible, given these, to work for better copyright protection. It is these aspects I wish to examine from the point of view of India.

Historical background

India is today signatory to both the Berne Copyright Union and the Universal Copyright Convention. In addition, its own copyright law, framed in 1957 was amended in 1984 and again in 1992. India's first entry into the world of international copyright was as a dominion of Britain, and it was therefore bound by the law of the 'mother country.' In this, it was no different from other colonized countries.

In the early 1960s, as more and more countries began to become independent, this situation gradually changed. As independent nations, many erstwhile colonial countries wished to set up their own educational programs, and to provide textbooks at locally affordable prices. But, because of the systematic depletion of resources, both material and intellectual, by the colonial powers, very few countries were in a position to do this and to develop local authorship. Competition from foreign books was fierce: not only had they been around for some considerable time, but they also carried with them the stamp of the 'foreign article' and were often seen as 'better' and 'more prestigious' than locally written and produced books. (In India for example, it had been a conscious policy with the colonial government to present English books as 'superior' and 'more reliable' than Indian ones). Despite pressure from local and indigenous publishers, foreign publishers were unwilling to give up what had become lucrative markets. This was particularly true of India, which presented a large and growing market for textbooks to publishers from the West. However, there was a growing feeling among developing nations that they needed intellectual resources, which were often only available from the West, and that it was wrong for educational programs to be deprived of such materials because of copyright restrictions. If Western publishers were not willing to make such books available, then local publishers should have the right to reprint them. [2]

In 1971, India took the lead in international negotiations on this tricky question. Over a three week period, representatives of both international copyright conventions met in Berne in parallel, often difficult, meetings, and what finally emerged was an agreement on what has come to be known as compulsory licensing. Compulsory licensing related to educational books, and enabled publishers (and the state) in developing countries to get a license to print a particular book in the country concerned, at a price that was reasonable for the local market. The granting of the license was contingent on the original copyright holder's being unable to make available such a work in the developing country. In addition, even in this event, publishers in developing countries had to wait for some considerable periods of time, before they could print the book under license.[3] The rights of the authors were protected at least in economic terms: that is, while anyone who printed a book using the compulsory licensing provision, was obliged to pay the author a royalty, the author did not have the right to refuse to license an edition of his or her work in a particular place.

Compulsory licensing was a hard fought gain: and one that had a place in the ideological terrain. It was the developing countries' way of correcting what they perceived as an historical imbalance. It is important to note that at no time were such licenses intended to deprive authors of their earnings, and the fear of them, on the part of developed countries, was founded not on the basis of copyright infringement, but rather on that of loss of revenue. The Publishers' Association in Britain, for example, was so concerned about this that it issued a detailed note to all its members, instructing them on how to deal with applications for compulsory licensing. The entire burden of the note was one of concern at the possible loss of a major market, and publishers were advised to attempt to make books available cheaply rather than let them go under license. Under Item 2. Compulsory Reprint Licensing, the Publishers' Association in its note on India: Compulsory Licensing stated that:

> By including this provision [i.e. compulsory licensing] in the Act, the aim has been to make available low-cost Indian reprint editions. *This is perhaps the aspect of the Act of most concern to British publishers, who have hitherto regarded India as a major export market for both trade and academic books.*[4] (my italics)

Where India was concerned, these fears were unfounded: there has not, till the present day, been even a single application for a book to be printed under compulsory license. What is particularly interesting for our purposes is that while India fought hard for the ideological victory of compulsory licensing at an international level, within the country it took nearly thirteen years before legislation could be amended to allow for applications for license. That is, the copyright law within India needed amendment to take in licenses, and this only happened in August 1984, with the Copyright (Amendment) Act 1983 coming into force.[5]

Why, after having fought for licensing, did India take so long to amend its own legislation? In the answer to this question lies one of the other key dilemmas of copyright: the gap between international agreements and legislation on the ground. I will come back to this later when I speak about territorial rights. For the moment, I would like to point out that one of the main reasons why publishers within India did not pressurize the State to bring compulsory licensing into force lies in the state of the Indian publishing industry.

In the early 1970s, Indian publishing, particularly in English, was well set for growth. At independence the process of 'Indianisation' had begun, with foreign publishing houses being allowed to stay, but only subject to a maximum shareholding of 49 per cent, and expatriate employees being phased out. (The only exception to this was Oxford University Press which continues to be a wholly owned subsidary of Oxford University Press, England). There was still a great need for textbooks, and much of the market dominated by the 'Western' article. A fairly liberal import policy allowed for the import of unlimited numbers of foreign books, provided they fell into the category of 'educational, scientific and technical books'; and a sizable, and secure (especially in terms of repatriation of foreign exchange) market allowed for these books to be priced lower than their home editions, though still not as cheaply as if they had been produced locally. Given that the country had a reasonable infrastructure in terms of printing technology, paper and binding, it soon became possible to produce many such books locally, either by Indian publishers, or by onetime foreign-owned Indian companies such as Orient Longman, Macmillan and others. Additionally, at the time, three major foreign subsidy schemes—the Joint Indo-American Textbook Program, the English Language Book Society and the Joint Indo-Soviet Textbook Program—ensured the availability of foreign texts at low prices. Another important factor was the fact that local publishers could, if they wished to, license the right to publish a book locally from a Western, usually American or British, publisher, provided the latter agreed. Thus, the situation which could have made compulsory licensing a necessity, did not actually exist on the ground, or at least did not have such urgency. The ministry dealing with applications reports that they had a bare three or four applications over several years, and even these were not followed through. Another reason was the bureaucracy involved in making applications, and the time limits stipulated as waiting periods for the different kinds of books.[6] All of these made compulsory licensing inoperative even before it began. Nonetheless, in spirit, the victory won at Berne was an important one, and even though Indian publishers have not used this provision, the moral point that was made at Berne has been an enabling one for other countries whose resources may not stretch as far as India's.

Today, things are somewhat different in India. The recent move to liberalize the economy has meant that foreign publishing houses can now enter into collaborative arrangements with Indian houses, without a limit of 49 percent being put on their shareholding. Thus, compulsory licensing is even more meaningless today, in actual terms, than it was in the seventies, although this does not negate its political significance. In addition, other factors have entered the picture.

Due to a phased process of nationalization carried out by the Indian government, a substantial part of school textbook publishing is now in the hands of the State. Syllabi have been standardized, and private publishers now hold only a small—albeit very lucrative—segment of the school textbook market. On other fronts, however, the Indian publishing industry has developed at a fairly rapid pace. Academic and trade publishing in English is in a healthy situation, with more and more books being published and exported. This is equally true of publishing in the fields of science, technology, medicine, and that most difficult of areas, children's books. While English continues to command the majority of the market, and the bulk of the resources, publishing in Indian languages has also grown.

Over the years the balance of exports and imports has also changed. While the volume of imports into India still continues to exceed exports, there is now a growing domestic market for different kinds of books. Publishers still complain that Indian authors prefer to be published outside the country, mainly in the West, but the truth is that more and more Indian writers are choosing to publish in India, and be exported if possible. Being a major producer of knowledge, India is now in a position of needing to protect that knowledge, and its copyright laws have recently been made more stringent. For example, until recently a civil offense, copyright now is a criminal offense and violators can be jailed. It is clearly in India's self interest to act in the interest of copyright protection, but despite this unquestionable reality, India continues to be suspect as a pirating country.

The Question of Piracy

At the start of this essay, I spoke about the issues which have been part of the debate on copyright. A great deal of cultural and historical baggage has accompanied these. Among countries of the 'developed' world, for example, there has been increasing concern at the question of piracy on the part of 'developing' countries. India has not escaped this fate: despite its rapidly developing publishing industry, India continues to be seen as a country from whom the West has a great deal to fear in terms of piracy. This assumption is based more on a belief that only the West has intellectual property to offer that is worth pirating than on any ground reality. A country such as India, which is in a position of being a major producer of knowledge, has much to lose by pirating, and a great deal to gain by abiding with international laws and agreements. Many Indian publishers feel that the continuing image, in the West, of India as a pirating country, has to do more with the fear of a loss of markets (India has, after all, been one of the most major markets for British and American publishers, a situation which may well change now that indigenous Indian publishing is on the upswing), than with the ethics of the issue.

There is no denying that there was a time when books published in the developed world were being pirated in developing countries, and in India too there were a few unscrupulous publishers who pirated books. However, what is often forgotten in debates such as this is that while not denying that piracy can, and does, exist, neither the Indian government nor associations of Indian publishers have ever condoned piracy, or excused it on ideological grounds. Indeed, so concerned has the publishing industry been about the danger of piracy, that in the early 1980s, the Federation of Publishers and Booksellers Associations in India took the initiative to form a joint anti-piracy unit along with the Publishers Association of Great Britain. This unit was located in Delhi and a lawyer experienced in copyright matters was retained to deal with cases. Book piracy of the foreign article, so to speak, has been considerably reduced in India partly because of the open import policy of the government, but also because, over a period of time, Indian books are beginning to occupy the Indian market, and both institutional and individual buying patterns are changing.

Interestingly, while India argued on behalf of developing countries in 1971, it is today in a rather vulnerable position itself. Its publishing industry is much more developed than that of its neighbors, for example, and both compulsory licensing, or indeed piracy, can be directed at India in much the same way as India directed the former at the West. Much more than pirating material from the West, India needs to worry about the threat of piracy from within, and sometimes from across the borders.

This takes many ingenious forms. While there is no way reports of such piracy can be confirmed, their existence, and functioning, is open knowledge among publishers in India. One of the provisions of the anti-piracy clauses in the copyright act is that pirated books can be seized, but this presupposes actually locating them. The imaginative pirate is able to get round this by storing books in places such as railway warehouses, keeping them constantly moving from one area to another, and getting them direct from such warehouses to selling agents.

In Delhi currently, a case is being argued in the courts which throws a different light on the question of piracy. Trade books published by an Indian subsidiary of a U.K. based publisher have been printed by a local publisher, who is himself a lawyer and who has carefully studied the copyright act to find the exact loophole that can suit him. When brought to court, this lawyer argued, convincingly where the judge was concerned, that while the Indian subsidiary had a general power of attorney to publish local editions of books by their U.K. principals, they do not hold any power of attorney that is specific to the titles in question. This may sound strange but copyright legislation is Kafkaesque at the best of times. Because copyright is now a cognizable offense, the offending publisher was initially jailed and then released on bail. Whatever stocks could be tracked down were also seized. But it was when the case came to court that the Kafka-like episode began: in court the complainant is required to prove his/her bonafides. He needs to prove his locus standi as 'owner' or sub-licensee of the work in question by showing the chain of assignments and licenses that has led from the original owner to him. For these, specific documents are required from the original publisher which cannot be produced instantly. Meanwhile, theoretically, if the offending publisher can afford to do so, he can simply reprint the same books again, and be booked, jailed, bailed, tried, and start all over again.

Publishers have stressed again and again that piracy is a problem that must be confronted on all fronts. The law itself is not enough to tackle the clever pirate, who can always find a way to evade its reach. As Pravin Anand, leading copyright lawyer and expert in India said at the 1992 IPA convention:

> Copying a book is similar to stealing somebody's jewelry. Large scale organized copying is like robbing a jeweler's shop or a bank. But then, there is a major difference. In the case of a bank robbery the newspapers are full of sensational news and the whole might of the State, especially the police, jumps in to catch the culprit; there is pressure of public opinion even on the judge trying the case. The effect is electric.
>
> On the other hand, in the case of a book pirate, the police justify their inaction by pointing to murder dockets; the State deflects the desperate appeals of copyright owners with nonchalance and the judge sits with a 'so what' attitude while the man on the street remains in stark oblivion.[7]

It is precisely because neither the buyer nor the law enforcer thinks there is something actually wrong in copyright infringement: for the law it is not an offense that is in any way tantamount even to a simple theft. For readers, it is not really an offense if they are doing it because they are doing what no one will argue with, saving money, and not being 'exploited' by business houses. And for the pirate, it matters little whether it is an offense or not. It is interesting that readers or scholars would not generally apply the same arguments to plagiarism of their work as they do to copyright infringement. Litigation, imprisonment, and seizing of stocks are hardly effective ways to counter piracy. At an international level, these methods are also expensive and time consuming. For those countries for whom piracy is a real problem, licensing reasonably priced local reprints is one of the necessary and effective methods of countering pirates.

The question of territorial rights

Inextricably tied in with the question of copyright is that of territoriality. The division of the world into territories for the purpose of copyright had, at one time, to do with the old established patterns of power. In the early days, territories as far apart as the U.K., Australia, India, and Canada were often tied together under the rubric of the Commonwealth. Geographical proximity had little meaning. Today, much of this has changed: old boundaries such as the 'Commonwealth and dependencies' or 'U.S.A. and scheduled territories' have little meaning; rather, territories are often sold individually, although with the removal of boundaries within the European community, and the breakup of the Soviet Union, this question has acquired fresh complications.

Although copyright and territoriality are tied to each other, they also often work at odds with each other. Thus, while the U.S. and India are both signatories to the Universal Copyright Convention which should, legally, protect their works in each other's territories, in actual fact this is not the case. Within the U.S. the existence of the Anti-Trust Law (also known as the Sherman Act) means that while a publisher may have sold the rights of a particular book to, say, a publisher in India, and technically the market for the U.S. edition of this book should then be closed as far as India is concerned, in actual fact, this does not happen. Under the provisions of the Anti-Trust Law, no conditions can be put on the resale of books from the United States. This effectively gives the U.S. license to infringe territorial arrangements with impunity, while at the same time maintaining its image as an international copyright 'hawk'. Given below are examples of a few key cases relating to international copyright which help illustrate the complexities of this issue.

The Penguin-India Book Distributors Case

In 1983 Penguin Books (England) brought a case against India Book Distributors, Delhi for infringement of Penguin's territorial copyright in 23 books. According to the suit, India Book Distributors were illegally importing into India and selling copies of books purchased in the United States but for which territorial rights for India were with Penguin Books (England). In the initial stages Penguin's request for an injunction (according to Indian law, copyright infringement at the time was a civil offense), was granted, but later it was vacated in the High Court and the offending party was asked to render account. Penguin then appealed and the injunction was reinstated through an interlocutory judgment. The reason for the initial vacation of the injunction was that the U.S. Government had, at one time, brought a suit against several British and American publishers (this included Penguin) on the basis that their agreements were in breach of the Anti-Trust Laws of the U.S. The Indian judge took the view that because Penguin was part of this suit, they therefore knew that they could not prevent any purchaser of lawfully published books in America from exporting these to India. He said: "On a plain reading of the clauses, it is clear that liberty is given to any purchaser in any part of the world to purchase lawfully published books in America and to export them wherever he likes." [8]

Penguin then took this case to the High Court of India, where the injunction was reinstated. In his order the judge held that whatever America's laws may be, they could have no extra-territorial effect. He asserted that no court could pass a decree that would affect the rights of persons outside its jurisdiction, thus the U.S. court's decree applied only within the boundaries of the U.S. and could not be used as an excuse by the Indian distributors, IBD. In his words: "The writ of the United States does not run in this country." He held that the importer of the books in question was subject to the laws of the country within which he was based. He said: "Copyright law is a territorial concept and each nation has its own laws. In America it may not be possible to place restrictions on the resale of books. But sale within the United States obviously cannot abrogate the effect of the laws of the particular place where they are imported." [9]

A second argument that was taken by India Book Distributors was that because what they were importing "lawfully published books" from the U.S. into India, there was no copyright infringement involved. To this the judge responded that the expression "owner of copyright" in the India Copyright Act (Section 54 (a)) included an exclusive licensee. [10]

This positive judgment was, however, only an interlocutory one and eventually the case would have had to come up for arguments in the Supreme Court of India. In the event, the two parties settled the matter out of court. For our purpose, however, what is important here is the issues involved. What, we might ask, is the value of international agreements to protect each other's intellectual property, if local laws work against them? As well, how can the two different perspectives in this kind of case be reconciled: for Penguin this was a market which they had legitimately 'bought'. For IBD, it was a market into which they could legitimately 'encroach,' quoting a U.S. law as the rationale. Yet, why should those copies have been 'legitimately' sold into a market that was technically closed?

The India Today case

A more recent case, once again relating to the U.S. and India, but in a somewhat reverse situation of the above, is also of interest. Although the case relates to magazines, the provisions being drawn upon are those of copyright conventions. A well-known Indian newsmagazine, *India Today*, is published in India in two editions, a domestic edition and an international one. The domestic edition is cheaper, carries domestic advertisements, and is meant for distribution at home, while the international one carries international advertising and is meant for sale abroad. Recently, *India Today* brought a case against a U.S. based Indian company, Peekay International, that was importing copies of the domestic edition of the magazine into the U.S. and selling them there. *India Today*'s stand was that not only was this an infringement of copyright and territoriality, it also resulted in a loss of market for them. The United States New York District Court's judgment is worth quoting at some length:

DISCUSSION

The United States and India are both signatories to the Berne Convention and the Universal Copyright Convention. Both conventions provide for works copyrighted in signatory foreign countries to be given copyright protection under United States law. It is not contested that the Domestic Edition of *India Today* is covered by both the Berne Convention and the Universal Copyright Convention....

The United States Copyright Act provisions dealing with the subject of importation are as follows. 17 U.S.C. S 501 (a) provides:

(a) Anyone who...imports copies of phonorecords into the United States in violation of Section 602, is an infringer of the copyright or right of the author as the case may be.

The section goes on to provide that the copyright owner may institute an action for infringement. 17 U.S.C. S 602 (a) provides:

(a) Importation into the United States, without the authority of the owner of the copyright under this title, of copies or phonorecords of a work that have been acquired outside the United States, is an infringement of the exclusive right to distribute copies or phonorecords under Section 106, actionable under Section 501.

Section 106 (3) provides, in pertinent part, that a copyright owner has the exclusive right to "distribute copies...of the copyrighted work to the public by sale." It is clear that the plaintiff is the "owner of the copyright" within the meaning of S 602(a) by virtue of its Indian copyright and the conventions. Plaintiff has copyright protection under United States law against defendants' unauthorized importation and distribution of the Domestic Edition of *India Today*. [11]

Thus, the United States District Court has, in no uncertain terms, restrained Peekay International from importing into the U.S. the domestic edition of *India Today*. One might ask whether, given international copyright agreements, two different criteria can be applied to different countries? Why should it, for example, be impossible to put restrictions on the export of American books because of the provisions of the Sherman Act, but at the same time, the reverse is not possible, and imports into the U.S. can be restricted? The anomaly is clear, and shows how difficult the area of territorial boundaries is: the United States law is patently in violation of international agreements, but remains in force. How then, can the same country present itself as an upholder of the ethics of copyright?

Another Indian publication, *Stardust*, brought a similar action against an Indian distributor, Central News Agency. Although the case is still being fought in the Indian courts, effectively, the Indian distributor has been restrained from selling the domestic edition of *Stardust* in the U.K. While, in such cases, both sides have their own logic, there are other elements to such questions that tend to get marginalized. In this particular case Central News Agency argues that restrictions on distribution of the Indian edition of the magazine outside India deny readers their rights. They point out that the magazine has readers in many parts of the world: by disallowing the sale of the Indian edition outside India, and with the foreign edition being printed only in the U.K. it is the rights of these readers that are denied. Why should a reader, say in Africa, have to buy a copy of *Stardust* from London rather than from India?

In the examples below, I will examine other, related, dimensions of the problem of territorial boundaries.

Copyright Between India and its Neighbors

This example relates to agreements arrived at between India and Pakistan. I use this to illustrate how geo-political concerns on the ground can and do militate against existing international agreements, and how, given these, copyright cannot be seen as an egalitarian concept that is somehow free of a political context. Because of their past history, India and Pakistan did not, by and large, enter into the kinds of reciprocal trade agreements that are common internationally. Thus there was no legal way, for example, that books published in India could be exported to Pakistan, or vice versa. Often, publishers would do this by taking rather circuitous routes: publish in India, export to Singapore, from where a local company would export to Pakistan. The export would then become legitimate. In 1988, however, the two countries signed a protocol under which trade in certain specified items could be carried on. This included books. Although the protocol was initially signed for a two-year period, it has not been repealed, and therefore continues to be in use. The Singapore route for books is therefore no longer necessary.

Despite this, however, copyright laws between India and Pakistan work against this opening up. Again, though both countries are signatory to international conventions, the Pakistan Copyright Act (titled The Copyright Ordinance, 1962, recently amended and made much more stringent) specifically states in the commentary to Chapter 1:

> Copyright in India is not applicable to Pakistan and vice versa. When India was partitioned the (English) Copyright Act, 1911, as modified by the Indian Copyright Act, 1914, became applicable to both countries but the two countries became foreign countries for each other, and there being no Order-in-Council relating either to India or to Pakistan, copyright having its origins in one country was deprived of protection in the other. Copyright of Indian origin is not recognizable in Pakistan and the same is the position with respect to the copyright of Pakistan origin in India. India has now repealed the Act of 1911 and has enacted the Copyright Act of 1957, but the last-mentioned Act has not affected the situation in relation to Pakistan. [12]

Thus, although books can now be exported and imported to and from both countries, and both belong to international conventions, there should logically be mutual protection. On the ground, however, the situation is different: there is no reciprocity for the simple reason that the Copyright Act, as it existed on 13 August 1947, was not ratified by either Pakistan or India and, therefore, there is no instrument of law. The question of copyright, therefore, is not one that can be separated from either history or current geo-political realities.

It can be argued, with some justification, that although both India and Pakistan come under the rubric of 'developing' countries, and theoretically they should be allies, in reality all developing countries are not equal or the same. Where publishing is concerned, for example, India is in a much stronger position than Pakistan: not only is its industry much more developed, but authorship, raw materials, and professionalism all place it in a better position—particularly where English language publishing is concerned. Is Pakistan—whose need for certain kinds of books is real—therefore not justified in taking such books from its better off neighbor?

With Bangladesh, India's other neighbor, the problems are somewhat different. Here, the reality of the situation is that there is a shortage of books in Bangladesh, and there is a tremendous (understandable) resistance, on the part of Bangladesh publishers to what they see as a threat: the possibility that their market will be "flooded" with Indian books. Notwithstanding this, the need for books cannot be denied, and according to Indian publishers, a kind of "legitimate piracy" has now become common. Neel Khot in Dhaka is a photocopying market with several hundred photocopying machines running "bookshops," providing instant photocopied books to students for a small price. Many of these are · Indian books. Indian publishers also claim that Indian texts are typeset onto acetate or tracing paper in Bangladesh and brought into India and printed. These then go out of the country as legitimate exports, exported by a local company.

Nepal provides a different example. Between India and Nepal, there are no trade barriers. In theory, if a Nepal based publisher were to license the rights for a particular book from, say, a U.K. based publisher, just for the Nepal market, this book could easily, and legally within trade agreements, find its way to India, even though the Indian market may theoretically be closed.

I have cited above only a few of the many copyright litigation cases, and have looked at anomalies between the laws of particular countries. It has been pointed out time and again that one of the key problems with copyright is the problem of enforcement. Another, which the above amply demonstrates, and which becomes clearer with the newer international agreements such as GATT, is that although in theory, international agreements relating to copyright are premised on the equality of nations, in reality this can never work, because there is no such equality, and there is no way copyright can be kept pure and apart from politics.

A Multiplicity of Rights

It is a truism to say the situation is a complicated one, and that it gets more complicated almost by the day. Photocopying, for example, has posed a major threat to copyright. At a session on copyright at the International Publishers Association meeting in Delhi in 1992, one of the main resolutions read: "Infringement of copyright arises in many cases from lack of public understanding of the notions of copyright."[13] All publishers know that the proliferation of small and large photocopying establishments all over the world, as well as the presence of photocopiers in libraries and other places, have meant a considerable loss of revenue. The question, however, is how to create public understanding of the ethics of the issue. In Third World countries there are other, practical and material, problems that attach to the issue. What argument can one offer, for example, to a relatively poor student in a developing country to whom the difference between buying and photocopying a book can often be as much as a month's rent? How does one even begin speaking of the ethics of the issue? Further, even if students were to be convinced that photocopying without permission were wrong, what advice would one offer to someone if a book is simply not available commercially because of territorial or distribution arrangements? It is because of this that even today, developing countries continue to reaffirm the need for cheap editions of textbooks and other educational materials. The availability of these can make an effective starting point to contain copyright infringement through photocopying.

Photocopying is not a problem that relates only to developing countries. As Ralph Oman, U.S. Register of Copyright, said at Delhi: "these suggestions [relating to enforcement of laws] apply with equal force to problems in developing countries. After all, unauthorized copying of copyrighted works is hardly unknown in the United States....Human beings can rationalize almost anything, and for those who want to be able to freely—and I use the word in both of its meanings—reproduce materials, the lack of an efficient, inexpensive clearance mechanism is reason enough to justify copying without permission."[14] Another important element with photocopying is that for the first time, publishers are having to deal, not with publishers in the matter of copyright infringement, but with their readers. How can you bring legal action against someone who is, in very real terms, your bread and butter? Hence the importance of educating and making people aware. Despite being disseminators of ideas, this is something publishers have never been particularly good at. In a country like India, unless you are a textbook writer, the kind of earning you may make from royalties is minimal. Most authors will complain—and many with reason—that they seldom get paid. For the general reader, this is a much easier thing to believe than that publishers work on tight budgets. Thus, for publishers to argue on behalf of authors' rights (as is often done in cases of photocopying) is something that does not carry much weight.

If photocopying posed problems of one kind, changes in technology have posed another. At an international level, copyright conventions have been amended to take in protection for computer programs, etc. Under the Trade Related Intellectual Property agreements (TRIPS) computer programs will be protected under the Berne Convention. Databases and other similar compilations of material also merit protection, if they can be said to come under the rubric of an 'intellectual' creation. With each new technological development, the old actors in the game of copyright enforcement—publishers, authors, distributors, supported by their governments—will get further distanced, and will be less in control. Not only will high speed new technology make any kind of enforcement difficult, but with the new agreements which focus on removing trade barriers, the advantage will very squarely be placed back in the hands of the more powerful countries. [15]

It is clear that the removal of trade barriers under the General Agreement on Trade and Tariffs (GATT) will go against the interests of the less developed countries. Until such times as markets are protected, the possibility of growth for publishers in the less powerful countries will continue to exist. With the opening up of markets, those with more access and money will come to dominate once again, and the old patterns of the flow of information, from north to south, east to west, which developing countries have been fighting against, will be reasserted. For open markets to be really 'open' there must be equality of resources and opportunity. Because these do not exist, markets can never be fully open in the real sense of the term. Another danger is that of the formation of cartels or trade blocs. For example, if booksellers and publishers in Europe, which is now a common market, were to decide that they would not allow books from X African publisher into their markets, there is little that publisher could do about it. This is why there is such concern about GATT in some developing countries.

With territoriality being such a vexed question for book publishers, it will be interesting to see what the future holds. With the GATT the powerful nations are arguing for the removal of boundaries and trade barriers. Although the entire discussion of Trade Related Intellectual Property Rights seems to have been couched in a language that has little to say about books, it nonetheless raises important questions for the future of books. In many ways, this removal of barriers will work against territorial rights, and may, in fact, result in widespread availability of different editions of books without regard to territoriality. In the words of Ralph Oman:

> International trade in intellectual property products is also dependent, from a publisher's perspective, on the ability to license territorially restrictive exclusive rights.... Paradoxically, then, the existence of a single world market would be undesirable for publishers, at least if one feature of such a market is dissemination of lawfully made copies without regard to territorial licenses. [16]

Another paradox is that while such 'free trade' will make different editions available and make a mockery of territoriality, it will, interestingly enough, serve the interests of readers who will have a choice, and wide availability. At the same time, it will, inevitably, serve the interests of the more rich and powerful as they will have the means and wherewithal to make cheaper copies available worldwide, and to promote them.

I have tried to show above some of the difficulties involved in the actual functioning of copyright at many levels. It is my belief that for any discussion to move forward, the old dichotomies of 'us' and 'them' will have to be done away with. It is only when this becomes a precondition that a genuine dialogue will begin. For this to happen, countries need to be aware of the complexities of the play of history, economics and politics on the ground, and to understand that the interplay of these forces can often create a situation of flux which, in turn, can have a direct bearing on how national and international laws are understood and implemented.

It is also important to understand that in the final analysis the discussion on copyright is a discussion about money, and no one is going to be willing to give that up easily. If there are two sides to the picture, they are made up of those who have money and those who don't: the former are naturally reluctant to give up what have long been 'their' markets, while the latter naturally want the field clear so they can develop their markets. A statement from Ralph Oman's speech on copyright at the International Publishers Association Conference in Delhi (1992) is apposite here. He says: 'Let's be blunt, all nations and all companies act in their own self-interest... if a concern for a nation's self interest isn't taken into account, can we realistically expect that nation to act in a manner that will bring economic benefit only to foreigners and at the expense of its citizens?'[17]

ACKNOWLEDGMENTS
I am grateful to Professor Philip Altbach for suggesting I work on this subject. Several of my friends and colleagues have been more than generous with both information and their time and I would like here to particularly thank Zamir Ansari of Penguin Books India and U.K., Arvind Kumar, Director of the National Book Trust, India, Sujit Mukerjee, ex-Director, Orient Longman, India and Jagdish Sagar, previously Books Officer, Ministry of Human Resource Development, Government of India. I am also grateful to Mohinder Dhillon of the Copyright office in India for his help in locating materials.

71

Notes

[1] *Rights*, vol 6, 1 (1992): my italics.

[2] "Copyright in Developing Countries," in *Priorities and Planning for the Provision of Books*, Report of the Commonwealth Asia-Pacific Regional Seminar (London: Commonwealth Secretariat 1973), 178-85.

[3] "The Overseas Copyright Committee, India: Compulsory Licensing," (The Publishers Association, London, 1985), 4. Time periods specified here are as follows: (a) seven years for fiction, drama, poetry, music or art, (b) three years for natural or physical sciences, math and technology, (c) five years for all other categories.

[4] "The Overseas Copyright Committee, India: Compulsory Licensing," (London: The Publishers Association, 1985), 4.

[5] Interestingly, compulsory licensing did not relate only to books, and in other areas, such as pharmaceuticals, it was extensively used. Today, in the discussions on the General Agreement on Trade and Tariffs (GATT) it continues to form a major part, particularly in relation to non-literary products. This, however, is outside the purview of this essay

[6] See note 3 above.

[7] *Rights*, vol. 6, 1 (1992), 6.

[8] High Court of Delhi, Judgment of August 1984 in the matter of Penguin Books Limited and M/s India Book Distributors and ors. 3-4.

[9] *Ibid*, 4.

[10] *Ibid*, 10.

[11] Judgment of the United States District Court Southern District of New York in the case of Living Media Limited, Plaintiff, against Harshad Parekh, Binoti Parekh, Peekay International Inc. and Sinha Trading Co. Inc., Defendants.

[12] *The Copyright Laws*, printed by Ch. Abdul Sattar (Lahore, 1992), 9. 13.

[13] *Rights*, vol. 6, 1 (1992), 5.

[14] *Ibid*, 4.

[15] Ralph Oman makes this point in ibid, above.

[16] *Ibid*, 3.

[17] *Ibid*.

Chapter 5

COPYRIGHT IN THE CHINESE CONTEXT

Janice Wickeri

Copyright has had a chequered history in China. For much of the present century, copyright protection in China has been short-lived or non-existent. The Qing dynasty law, adopted in 1910, fell in 1911 along with the dynasty. A new copyright law was passed by the Kuomintang in 1928, and was abrogated by the Communist victory, though given the social and political disruptions of the KMT years, it was never very effective in any case. After 1949, the idea of "intellectual private property" came under attack as much as other forms of private property. Though in the early years of the People's Republic, principles of author's rights were recognized, these were eclipsed (like many other facets of the law) by the rise of leftist radicalism—to enshrine copyright in law would have been a counter-revolutionary act.

Thousands of years of totalitarian rule had engendered in the populace an indifference to the law, an attitude little changed by the time the Communists rose to power. Add to this the further erosion of awareness of the law or the very existence of law itself by the Cultural Revolution, and it is hardly surprising to find a popular saying which sums up the received attitude with which authorities attempting to enforce new copyright laws must contend: "Every essay under the sun is a copy of every other essay." The corollary is, "If you know how to copy, you're original—if not, you're plagiarizing."

The traditional Chinese view of the right to exploitation of a work is thus opposite to the principle and spirit of copyright. Before China opened to the West in the late Qing dynasty, authors felt more honored the more their works were read and copied by other scholars. Yao Nai, a famous Qing dynasty essayist instructed his grandnephew thus: "...if before you imitate a master closely, you strive for originality, you are bound to achieve nothing at all. This is exactly the same as when one learns calligraphy: without copying a model, how can you succeed?"[1] Another old saying has it that when a particularly well-written piece of literature appears, the price of paper in Luoyang (an ancient capital of China) will soar: all the other scholars will be copying it. These traditional ideas made copyright a very difficult concept in China, Taiwan and Korea.

Chinese Copyright Law

Writing on intellectual property in China in 1986, Michael Pendleton hypothesized that China might work out an approach to copyright law based on its own history and approach rather than selecting among purely western options, and that it was possible given China's market potential that the nation might be able to withstand demands to recognize full foreign copyright.[2] A nation which in the sixties and seventies was seen as a leader among developing nations in resisting the pressures from developed countries for greater restrictions on access to technology and other forms of intellectual property, might have been expected to adopt a copyright law with "Chinese characteristics," features which mark it as quintessentially Chinese in contrast to laws passed by other, particularly western, nations. Certain provisions of the Chinese law do spring from local conditions or traditions, yet the law adopted in 1990, in general follows international copyright norms and is described by Chinese scholars as being formulated with close attention to international models.[3]

In the midst of the political and economic changes of the post-Cultural Revolution era, China's approach to copyright issues has greatly changed. The legal system, moribund during the Cultural Revolution, has begun to feel the effects of the new policies of reform and openness, particularly in areas affecting international economic relationships. The importance of international trade to China's rapidly expanding economy has meant that laws related to these areas are being modernized or newly formulated to provide a workable and acceptable framework for trade and for China's role in multinational accords, such as GATT. There is no debate at an official level, at least, in China over the appropriateness of copyright law, unless it would be among "die-hard leftists" who might see copyright as an incursion into the public domain where all property should be held in common among the people. Indeed, when the law was promulgated, some long-time cadres were heard to ask whether this was a socialist law or a capitalist one. But such remarks are noted in Chinese sources only to show that vestiges of outdated thinking exist. Copyright law is not seen on an abstract or idealistic plane as a limitation on access to knowledge, but pragmatically as a necessity in international business relationships important for modernization.

With one of the fastest growing economies in the world, though the pace and depth of development is uneven, China has become an attractive market and is in turn anxious to increase both its own exports and the scale of foreign investment. China sees itself as one of the great nations with an important role to play on the international scene. A 1991 article in the bilingual journal *China Patents & Trademarks* describes the official position:

> In order to better carry out our policy of opening to the outside world, promote the development of literature, art, science and technology, and the exchange and cooperation between China and foreign countries in the cultural, scientific, economic and commercial fields, China should normalize its foreign copyright relations as quickly as possible by getting in touch with WIPO and UNESCO to study the feasibility of accession to international copyright conventions and try to join international copyright conventions at the earliest date in order to play the role that China should play as a country with an ancient civilization, a great cultural nation, a developing country and a socialist country to contribute to international cooperation in the cultural, scientific and artistic fields.[4]

Thus, in 1992, within a few years of adopting its own Copyright Law, China joined both the Berne Convention and the Universal Copyright Convention. The adoption of the Chinese Copyright Law and the Implementation Regulations is seen as part of China's modernization process, part of the current policy of openness and reform.

The present Chinese Copyright Law evolved over a long period of study and consultation, during which other facets of intellectual property law, the Chinese Trademark Law (1982) and the Chinese Patent Law (1984) were adopted. Both laws broke new ground in socialist China by defining intellectual products as commodities. Even in the early 1980s, China had been moving in the direction of copyright protection; before the adoption of the Chinese Copyright Law, the Copyright Agency of China was set up to deal with permission for use of material from Taiwan and Hong Kong. Since the law was formulated with an eye to international intellectual property laws, many of its features are standard; its basic provisions are in line with those of Berne and in a number of instances provide higher levels of protection than those currently provided for in the UCC.

A certain few of its provisions bear mention. The Chinese law is generally felt to be biased in favor of the original author and author's rights, in contrast to U.S. or U.K. laws, which tend to emphasize the rights of the entrepreneur who exploits the work. In addition, both the economic and the moral rights of authorship are recognized, with quite broad provision for moral rights: the right of authorship, the right of alteration and the right of integrity are perpetual. Its prevailing spirit is much closer to the approach taken in the Berne Convention, rather than the more American approach reflected in the UCC. Features such as the author's exclusive right to authorize others to exploit the work, and receive remuneration from such exploitation are seen in China as following the socialist principle of distribution according to work. Chinese "characteristics" of the law may be the fact that unlike copyright laws in many other nations, there are no criminal penalties attached to serious infringement of the law, only civil liabilities, which may include fines. Copyright infringement is thus not considered as criminal theft. This is said to be necessary because the history of copyright protection in China is brief and time must be allowed for people's consciousness of the law to mature. This, however, is precisely what makes enforcement more difficult. In addition, as in Taiwan, it is up to the victim to bring the case and provide sufficient evidence. Policing, vigorous or not, as in Hong Kong, is not carried out by enforcement authorities. This situation makes pirating of books very difficult to control. The success of the Taiwan copyright law was the very strict sentence given: imprisonment plus fine.

The Copyright Law of China clearly states that in relevant disputes where the Chinese law conflicts with an international copyright agreement to which China is a signatory in providing less protection, the international agreement takes precedence, on the principle of minimum protection of conventions. If China rejoins GATT, it may have to adjust its practices or amend the law to accommodate the more serious penalties attached. Infringement disputes may be handled through arbitration or mediation or by litigation. The National Copyright Administration of China administers the law.

The Copyright law is unique in having "Rules on the Implementation of International Copyright Treaties" which were drawn up in response to American demands in the Sino-American Memorandum of Understanding agreed in June 1992. Though some Chinese commentators hold that China's acceptance of these Implementation Rules is proof positive of China's good faith in international agreements, others find them an irksome imposition and an indication that U.S. officials do not understand China's legal system. But it may be that the Rules serve at times to make the terms of the existing law more precise and more easily applied to specific cases, though both Chinese and foreign experts feel accession to further international accords, such as GATT, will necessitate extensive reforms to the law itself.

The adoption of the law was hailed domestically and abroad. Attention now focuses on implementation and enforcement. The law is still very new and the number of cases brought to the courts has as yet been insufficient to show up possible loopholes or identify trends in its application. Certainly the number of cases with international implications has been even fewer, but these have been swiftly dealt with. Rights of Taiwan authors have been upheld (see below) and very recently, Chinese composers successfully invoked the law against Japanese infringers of their rights.

The Chinese Context

Since adopting its policies of reform and openness, China has tended to provide swift attention to cases in which foreign companies or investors are involved. The way has at times been smoothed for foreign business interests by authorities at various levels, whatever national policy; at times at the expense of domestic interests or workers. This is of course one level of implementation and one set of relationships which the law is meant to address. The other level addresses domestic situations, the rights of Chinese citizens over the products of their intellectual labor within their own society. Continued successful implementation of the law on both these levels depends on the efficient working of the legal machinery, at present a very problematic area.

Legislation is currently being enacted at a rapid pace to service China's growing markets at home and participation in the global economy. As the *South China Morning Post* recently noted, the Chinese government is "rushing to establish a permanent legal framework to govern reformed trade practices..."[5] The framework of written law, however, must rely on efficiently run courts and well-trained lawyers. China faces difficulties in both these areas. There is a dearth of trained lawyers, not only because of the political legacy of times when law was a profession of remarkably low status, but because of a shortage of qualified law professors to train them. For decades after the establishment of the PRC, no attention was given to commercial, financial or corporate law, those areas which are rapidly expanding as foreign companies do business in China, and China expands its own involvements abroad. The state of the legal profession may not be a particular problem in the area of copyright. Literary agencies specializing in Chinese authors often offer legal services as well, and some courts are now setting up intellectual property divisions. However, the fact that copyright, patent and trademark law is administered separately continues to cause difficulties.

In spite of the emphasis on centralization of power in the socialist model, in practice, power and authority often become dispersed through the various levels of government, from national to provincial to county and so on, sapping efficiency and becoming mired in the difficulty of coordinating the different levels. Overstaffing, waste of staff energy and money and, as observed above, shortage of high level personnel plague the legal apparatus as they do other areas of official life in China, not only in terms of the court system, but in offices whose task it is to administer the law and oversee arbitration, mediation and so on, as well. "Now whenever a competent authority is created in respect of a certain field of intellectual property, dozens of local and derivative authorities are created almost simultaneously."[6] Such local authorities have a role, the author concedes, but should be simplified and merged where at all possible.

It has often been observed that the bureaucracy associated with Chinese officialdom throughout history is no less under socialism than it was under the emperors. To deal with the seemingly endless layers of authority, the culture developed an elaborate system of reliance upon a network of relationships and personal appeal, the much-maligned *guanxi* (relationship) system. Under this system, the person in a particular office or position becomes as, if not more, important than the authority of the office itself. This has been termed rule by personality, and, from the highest echelons of the Communist Party, where patriarch Deng Xiaoping continues to exert great influence and power, down to the incumbent of the neighborhood committee, tends to pre-empt or hinder rule by law. Thus, a reforming official can meet with obstacles at every turn, and citizens place their hopes upon honorable, sympathetic or merely complaisant office holders, rather than upon the tenets of the law. In the modernization process, awareness of the laws of the land must be learned and citizens and officials alike make a habit of submitting themselves to the legal process.

In rural areas of China, low levels of education further complicate the picture. In addition, the government may have been sending mixed signals about the pursuit of profits in its encouragement of farmers to take part in the China's economic boom. New habits of thinking about what is and is not allowed, new standards of judgment, must be formed and extended beyond the common sense and the politically acceptable. The "distribution" of a pirated edition of a primary-school textbook in Hebei is a case in point. *A Primary Student's Guide to Fifty Common Topics for Composition* was published in Beijing and promptly pirated by three publishers in two Henan counties. Peasants in the area were buying the pirated books wholesale and selling them at a profit. A representative of the Beijing publisher, sent to investigate, urged the farmers not to continue selling the books. They were taken aback: "After all, it's not a politically reactionary book and it's not pornography either. What law are we breaking?"[7]

Awareness and acceptance of the law may be a habit of citizenship which must be fostered at all levels of society. Adoption of a law is well and good; implementation of the law is something which must happen in the context of daily life. The shift to an ingrained way of thinking about what constitutes justice in society is evidently something which must be built up over time through public education as well as the gradual accretion of precedent. These are two factors, both of which are crucial in the situation China currently faces in its desire to establish secure copyright protection.

Chinese intellectuals, who might be expected to benefit most from the protection of intellectual property, have not been very active. They are seemingly traumatized by their treatment in the struggles of China's recent past. One writer traces the ambivalence toward intellectuals in China back to the various literary inquisitions of the imperial era.[8] During the Cultural Revolution era, efforts were made to foster collective anonymous authorship, examples of which can be found in *Chinese Literature*, an English-language literary journal published by the Foreign Languages Press in Beijing. In 1972, for instance, issue No. 2 carried a short story, "Look Far, Fly Far" written by the "Shanghai dockers' spare-time writing group." The rebuilding of both self-confidence and the concept of author's rights among those most affected by them is a slow process. Cases which highlight the low self-esteem and low social standing of intellectuals and their subsequent "weakness" and unwillingness to claim their rights in cases of copyright infringement are numerous. Established scholars may take advantage of students seeking their opinion on a thesis or paper by publishing the paper under their own names. One innocent soul felt flattered by plagiarism by a well-known figure, since it showed that his ideas must be worthwhile.[9] Publishing houses, which until recently have been state enterprises, have often dealt summarily with authors in matters of payment and royalties, making decisions based on their own benefit.

The case of Zhou Haiying versus the People's Literature Publishing House highlights both the position of intellectuals in society and the ambivalence many people feel toward an individual claiming his or her rights before the law, especially when financial gain is involved. When Mr. Zhou, son of Lu Xun, generally acknowledged as China's greatest Twentieth century writer, who died in 1936, took the publisher to court in the 1980s seeking the balance of monies (some RMB 270,000) owed from his fathers' works, which had been "temporarily" deposited in the publishers' accounts, he was widely criticized for his presumption. What did he want so much money for? Though the government had rejected an offer made by Zhou and his mother in the 1950s to donate the money to national reconstruction, popular opinion in the 1980s felt he had gone back on his word. The case has still not been entirely resolved.[10]

The picture should not be presented as entirely bleak, however. Just as there are uneven levels of development economically, so are there varying levels of development in consciousness (for want of a better word), and success in applying the law, particularly in less politically sensitive areas such as copyright.

A case in point is perhaps the most celebrated copyright dispute thus far under the new law: that of the *Later Life of the Last Emperor*, a book about Aisin Gioro Puyi, the last Qing Emperor, by Chinese author Jia Yinghua. Charges were brought by Li Shuxian, Puyi's widow, and her collaborator, a researcher named Wang Qingxiang, who claimed that nearly seventy per cent of their joint work, *Puyi's Later Life*, had been plagiarized by Jia: in "theme, language, the setting out of chapters and sections and paragraphs, and the arrangement of historical facts."[11] It was also claimed that he had used Puyi's diaries, and Li's unpublished reminiscences without permission, infringing her copyright to those manuscripts as well. The plaintiffs demanded an immediate cessation of infringement, public apology, destruction of the published work and damages amounting to half the profits from its sale.

The case, tried in two Beijing courts, aroused great public interest, not only because of the parties involved and the drawing power of Puyi's name, but because of the way it was fought in court, with an enormous amount of detailed concrete evidence brought by the defendant which finally overwhelmed the plaintiff's case. The defense drew upon an up-to-date understanding of copyright in a way which was perhaps unprecedented in China at the time.

According to the report in the *Legal Daily*, the presentation of plaintiffs' rapid-fire arguments and the defense rebuttal took on the feeling of a ping-pong match, as Jia refuted claims of plagiarism with detailed comparisons of the two texts. One example of a disputed passage which the plaintiff claimed plagiarized their joint work will suffice:

> Puyi "sat at the window of the train compartment, waving at the people on the platform who had come to see him off. From the expression on his face, he seemed happy, he also seemed sad. It was with such contradictory emotions, that Puyi reluctantly left Fushun."from *Puyi's Later Life* ,last paragraph, p.25.

> "Among them was a tall robust man wearing yellow-framed glasses who had a particularly hard time keeping a grip on his emotions, first he cupped his chin in his hands, then he pulled out a pen and began writing something on a slip of paper. This special traveler, a man in his mid-fifties, was none other than China's last emperor—Aisin Gioro Puyi." from *The Later Years of the Last Emperor*, first paragraph, p. 5.

The defendant pointed out that he had given a vivid description of the man's emotional state, while the plaintiffs' book was content with the flat "contradictory emotions." He said charges based on such evidence transgressed the copyright law whose basic spirit was to protect the form, not the content, of the work.

Liu Chuntian, writing in the journal *China Patents & Trademarks,* cites this case as one demonstrating the "constantly increasing ability of Chinese courts to handle intellectual property cases." The case, he notes, was marked by a shift in past practices: particular attention was given to court inquiry concerning evidence and the standard of proof placed on the parties involved increased. This marked a change from the days when the court gathered a great deal of evidence but gave short shrift to examining evidence in court. Liu praised the decision as "more precise and normative."[12] These changes were not simply a function of this case, of course, but were made possible by the new civil procedure law.

Despite such successes, pirating of domestic works appears to be flourishing in China. *Ruined Capital* by Jia Pingwa, a best-seller in late 1993, had an official print run of 700,000 copies, quickly followed by pirate editions totaling some two million copies. When the book was banned as pornographic and proceeds impounded, the publishers, the state-affiliated Peking Press, supplied booksellers with pirate copies.[13] The bottom line was not law but profit, or perhaps there was poetic justice in breaking the ban with illicit copies. It would appear that nothing is sacred in the eyes of the book pirates. Barely a month after publication of Deng Rong's book about her famous parent, *Deng Xiaoping: My Father*, was published in September 1993, several publishers flooded the market with over 100,000 illicit clones.[14] Presumably given the vast potential market in China, multiple pirate editions still have a reasonable market. It may take some time and larger, better-organized publishers before unfettered pirating of the same title works to the disadvantage of potential pirates. Until this happens or the law fleshes out into real muscle, pirating, which extends even more seriously into CD's, video and film, will continue to be a lucrative business.

Translation Rights

Nearly all foreign works must past through the crucible of translation for use or sale in China. Unauthorized translations and pirated western (and presumably Asian, particularly Japanese) books abounded in the early eighties. Foreign teachers in China were aware of the "back rooms" of foreign languages bookstores where all sorts of things, including hard to come by textbooks could be had, though purchase of these was theoretically barred to foreigners. Chinese foreign language teachers moonlighted as translators of overseas bestsellers. Often western novels were being translated by individual translators for several different publishers, success (and remuneration) depending upon who made it into print first. As China moved toward establishing copyright, books were sometimes published first and regularized later. In October 1991, a book by Chinese-American Professor Zhang Wenwei was translated for publication by the Law Publishing House. Professor Zhang knew nothing of this at the time, but was informed by letter when the book was published. With the aid of a lawyer during a later visit to China, Prof. Zhang was able to reach an agreement for payment of royalties. I had a similar experience, receiving a letter from the Foreign Languages Press informing me that my translation of a short story had been included in an anthology and a permissions fee of some RMB 30 would be held for me until my next visit to Beijing.

The situation of course had its corollary overseas. Prior to the 1980s, China scholars, generally unable to contact Chinese writers for their permission, translated material at will, a habit which tends to persist on a certain level even today. However, more recently some authors have been well represented by their translators who have found publishers for them. As the international profile of Chinese literature increased, American and British literary agents began signing Chinese authors anxious to see translations of their work published overseas. In the early years, at least, inexperienced Chinese authors often lacked understanding of what such a contract entailed and continued to give verbal permission to various requests from independent translators. Literary agents, for their part, often failed to realize the situation in China and the lack of awareness of how business relationships worked overseas. Thus far it seems that, as far as literature is concerned, no particular work has been highly successful in terms of sales. Contemporary Chinese literature and Chinese authors have not yet become familiar to the American or English reading public, though a number of important novels or story collections have been translated and published.

It is more likely that mutual growth in translation rights will take place in non-literary areas of publishing. Chinese publishers such as the venerable Commercial Press have published translations of dictionaries and scientific and technical works as well as more popular nonfiction titles on business know-how, biographies etc. There are also projects to translate and publish in English works on Chinese art and related subjects.

In the late eighties, Chinese publishers began seeking translation rights for foreign works they wished to publish in China and entering into co-publishing agreements with foreign publishing houses. It has not always been easy for such activities to get off the ground. Though the *yuan* is now freely convertible, the costs of foreign rights remain high, especially as there has been a decline in book-buying as consumers spend their on consumer products other than books. The market is seen to be vast, but may be nearly uncontrollable, with a diffuse and unmanageable distribution system. The intricacies of international copyright law and bureaucratic inefficiency add to the problems for the Chinese purchaser of foreign rights. The brief life of copyright law in China in China so far means foreign sellers of such rights cannot be sure how cases will be played out in the courts, or how much muscle the law actually has domestically. Still, many overseas publishers seem optimistic about doing business in China. [15]

Taiwan and Hong Kong

A related area, that of Chinese language rights, has been transformed by the ascendancy of copyright law as well. Pirating was commonplace throughout the region, of course, and even after pirating of western books became less of a problem in Taiwan (moving on to Korea), Chinese-language books found their way across the straits and over the China-Hong Kong border. The traffic was two-way, with mainland, Taiwan and Hong Kong authors bearing the brunt of the losses. They were aware of what was happening, of course, but could do little to prevent it or to recover their losses. In the 1970s, important scholarly works by mainland authors found their way onto the shelves of Taiwan bookstores minus the author's name and provenance. With the changes in copyright in Taiwan and the implementation of the Chinese Copyright Law in 1990, this situation has been redressed; mainland authors sign contracts with Taiwan publishers for Taiwan editions of their books, or publish a work first in Taiwan or Hong Kong (this is especially true for politically sensitive writings) and Taiwan and Hong Kong authors contract for mainland editions of their works. Slowly, such deals have become a lucrative source of income for authors. Some intra-regional pirating is still said to exist, but at very low levels.

With copyright protection and the possibility of dealing directly with counterparts in whichever Chinese publishing community, this is an area which can be expected to grow substantially. Several agencies specializing in Chinese language rights now operate in the region and there is talk of the desirability of "world Chinese licenses".[16] That this is possible demonstrates the extent of changes taking place on the business and practical, if not the political, level over the years of the Chinese Open Door policy. With the advent of computers, a potential headache in marketing Chinese language books between mainland China and her Chinese-reading neighbors disappears. Changing simplified characters for the traditional variety and vice versa becomes a simple technical procedure. Since translations done on the mainland are generally considered to be better—and are cheaper to do—the licensing of traditional character rights or vice-versa increases market and sales potential.

With the mainland, Hong Kong and Taiwan currently set to become separate members of GATT, certain technicalities will have to be ironed out. Presently, mainland authors are seen by Taiwan as Chinese citizens "living under different systems," and as such are subject to the somewhat lower levels of protection provided by Chinese domestic copyright law. When China, Taiwan and Hong Kong are all separate members of GATT, it will be possible to have certain groups of Chinese citizens receiving higher levels of protection than the majority. Another interesting example arises from the provision in the Chinese copyright law concerning translation of works in Chinese into the minority languages of China (Article 22.sec.11). According to the law, permission does not have to be sought nor royalties paid to translate an already published work in Chinese into a minority language to be distributed in China, as this is considered fair dealing. Korean is one of the minority languages of China. If a Korean translator were to translate the work of a Taiwan author without permission and that work were to be imported into China or reprinted in China and distributed there, under the present law, this would not be considered a copyright infringement in China, however it might be seen in Korea. One could imagine an even more tortured process by which a bestseller overseas could be translated into a minority language.

Two exceptions have already been attached to the Implementing Regulations to deal with circumstances arising from this article. When China and Taiwan join GATT, a third may have to be added to deal with the hypothetical situation described above. For this reason and various other situations arising related to previously existing arrangements among the three or between one of the three and a third country, some within the mainland are calling for a revision of the Chinese copyright law to bring its provisions as much as possible into line with the international agreements.[17] Some conflicts arise simply because Taiwan embraced the copyright concept earlier than China and is ahead of it in certain areas of bilateral and multilateral agreements and trade.

In fact, mainland publishers have been seeking copyright permission from Taiwan authors since the late 1980s, and successful cases for redress of infringement have been brought.

The first case of copyright infringement brought in China on behalf of a Taiwan author involved the author Luo Lan and was settled in favor of the author and his mainland publisher. In 1988, Luo signed an agreement with the China Copyright Agency to represent the rights of all his works on the mainland. In 1988, a publisher in Shenzhen contracted for the rights and published Luo Lan's *Thoughts on Life* in two volumes. By June of 1990, a pirated edition had appeared in Beijing. After failing to reach any agreement with the publisher of the pirated edition, the Agency took the case to court on Luo's behalf in May 1991. After a year of deliberating the court ruled in the plaintiff's favor, ordering the various infringers involved to pay damages to Luo Lan of 18,900 RMB and 20,000 RMB to his publisher. An appeal by one of the defendants was rejected.[18]

The influence of Chinese copyright law and practices on other Chinese enclaves in the region, particularly Hong Kong and Macau, will continue to grow as these former colonies are reintegrated with the mainland. Hong Kong has a past reputation as a center for piracy, not so much for western language books as for luxury consumer products and computer software and manuals. Despite frequent raids and crackdowns on such practices, it is likely to remain a problem, as it is throughout the region. As long as ninety per cent of all software being used in China has been copied illegally, the production or importation of such products in Hong Kong is unlikely to stop.[19] Book publishing, except for the reproduction of computer manuals, is not a real problem, though there seems to be a somewhat casual attitude toward permission to reprint at times, particularly with regard to translations. Anthologies of Chinese or English poetry in a bilingual format, which are quite popular, have at times drawn rather freely on existing translations without having all their reprint permissions in order. Such practices may have gone relatively unnoticed in the past, but pose a definite problem today when these publications have a growing overseas market and in light of GATT. However, it is to be assumed that intellectual property issues as they affect Hong Kong will continue to focus on areas other than book publishing: those mentioned above, as well as the counterfeit CDs which abound in hawkers' stalls.

As a British colony, of course, Hong Kong has long had copyright laws (based on the 1956 British Act, though this has been superseded in the U.K.) and international agreements to which Britain has been a party have been extended to Hong Kong. As of this writing, moves are underway to revise the Hong Kong law, which is felt to be "outdated, complex and deficient...to deal with technological developments." The revisions are basically along the lines of the current (1988) British Act with certain local differences.

Of course as 1997 and Hong Kong's reversion to China near, efforts are being made to bring local laws into line with the draft Basic Law by which the Special Administrative Region (SAR) will be governed. In the copyright area it has meant drafting a Hong Kong ordinance to replace the U.K. Act. In the larger context, differences between Chinese and British views on the future structure of Hong Kong law and government have reached an acrimonious impasse. Given Hong Kong's intimate role in the economic miracle of southern China and Hong Kong's own booming economy, which owes a good deal of its continued health to that of its neighbor to the north, neither side appears to wish to see political issues undermine economic ones. Hong Kong wishes to be seen as the gateway to dealing with China and many local arms of international publishers base their Asia or China related activities here and pursue active programs with China, drawing on reputation for ability to ensure high quality. For Hong Kong, it is very important to retain its position of importance and not fall below international standards in the areas of trade and intellectual property. Thus, Hong Kong wants to be an independent and full party to the GATT agreement.

These hopes are posited on assurances from China that basically British-based institutions and laws, adjusted to meet the requirements laid out in the Basic Law, will continue post 1997. The question is to what extent this will be the case. There have been ongoing contacts between Chinese intellectual property authorities and the Intellectual Property Department of the Hong Kong Government. The *Report on Reform of the Law Relating to Copyright* of the Law Reform Commission of Hong Kong (1993) calls for existing international copyright and neighboring rights treaties to continue to apply to Hong Kong in their latest texts using a multilateral approach. The uncertainty is whether existing laws will continue to be applied, or whether the SAR will draft its own legislation. Adopting as far as possible the provisions of the 1988 U.K. law locally, it is felt, will allow Hong Kong to continue to draw upon the resources of English case law in further developing copyright law. However, some Chinese officials have hinted that English case law tradition should be scrapped in 1997, and the continental approach followed by China be adopted. Whether this is rhetoric or policy is not yet clear.

Conclusion

Many of the difficulties incumbent on the implementation and enforcement of copyright law in China are not unique to the area of copyright, but are rather the products of an inefficient administrative apparatus which plague so many areas of public life. To the extent that the various means by which China is run are reformed and modernized, there should be a gradual improvement in the workings of the legal process, particularly in areas which do not touch upon sensitive political issues. In the midst of rapid economic expansion and the temptations of the market place, it is no easy task to create recognition of intellectual property as an important and tangible human product to be protected from theft, and it is not only the greed of a few which makes it so.

However impressive the economic achievements taking place, they are uneven, and it will be some time before the benefits trickle to poorer areas of China still plagued by low levels of education and lack of basic medical care. A book of violin music recently purchased in Beijing, complete with ISBN number, obviously printed under license from the European publisher by China Music Publishers, sold for ten *yuan* (about US$1.15). This is much cheaper than a similar imported book in Hong Kong. Indeed the high book price of foreign publications is a disadvantage—in general, prices of commodities, including books, are very low compared to the outside world. Yet even ten *yuan* would be beyond the reach of certain sectors of the Chinese buying public and well beyond that of a music-loving peasant in Gansu. While China may wish to accommodate international agreements in the standards it sets for copyright and related intellectual property issues, it will also be important to protect related domestic industries and the distribution of their products to those who may need, but cannot afford them. Copyright affects not only business propositions, but larger social policy.

In the wrangling over Most Favored Nation trading status with the United States, and the drawn-out process of GATT approval, there have been defiant warnings by China that the country would consider abandoning the multilateral process in favor of bilateral arrangements with willing trading partners, rather than allow any other nations to influence either human rights or labor policies. Beneath and around what is surely to some extent rhetoric, there are signs that China is looking to ensure greater levels of protection for domestic products of intellectual endeavor. The case of Chinese computer software company SunTendy facing competition from Microsoft is an example.[20] It would be futile to attempt a last word on developments in copyright practice and intellectual property issues in the China region. Certainly the situation will continue to change and the future shape of copyright practice in China may be rather different than it is today.

Notes

[1] Yao Nai, "From a Letter to His Grandnephew Boang," translated by Frederick Tsai, *Renditions,* Nos. 41 & 42 (November 1994).

[2] Michael Pendleton, *Intellectual Property in China* (Singapore: Butterworth, 1986), p. 41.

[3] "Copyright Protection in China," *China Patents & Trademarks,* No. 2, 1991, 42-50.

[4] Liu Song, "On the Scope of Application of the Chinese Copyright Law," *China Patents & Trademarks,* No. 3, 1991: p. 44.

[5] *South China Morning Post,* February 8, 1994.

[6] Wang Zhengfa, "The Chinese Intellectual Property System at the Turning Point," *China Patents & Trademarks,* No. 1, 1992. 24-25.

[7] "Protection the Intellect," *Law and Life* [falu yu shenghuo], January 6, 1992. 42.

[8] Lai Xiaopeng, "Copyright Infringement and Copyright Laws," *China Law Reporter* No. 47, 1993, 71.

[9] Both examples, "Protecting the Intellect," 41.

[10] Liu, "The Current Situation," 78.

[11] *Legal Daily,* January 8, 1993.

[12] Liu, "The Current Situation," 80.

[13] Lincoln Kaye, "Reining in Erotica," *Far Eastern Economic Review,* November 18, 1993, 40-41.

[14] *Hong Kong Standard,* March 3, 1994.

[15] Sally Taylor, "The Opening of China," *Publishers Weekly* September 27, 1993.

[16] Sally Taylor, "The Opening of China." S19.

[17] Zheng Chengsi, "GATT and Copyright Across the Straits," *Social Sciences in China,* No. 1, 1994, 53.

[18] *Guangming Daily,* November 30, 1992.

[19] *South China Morning Post,* March 23, 1994.

[20] *China Daily Business Weekly,* April 3-9, 1994.

Chapter 6

COPYRIGHT—BENEFIT OR OBSTACLE?

Lynette Owen

My perspective on copyright is that of a publisher who has worked for more than twenty-five years in multinational educational and academic publishing houses. This sector of the publishing industry has broad experience of trading in international markets and as such has a keen awareness of the importance of copyright as a necessary background to trading in rights worldwide.

The Importance of Copyright

The concept of copyright is vital in that it provides the framework for creativity in a whole range of activities of which the written word is only one. Without the safeguards provided by copyright, there would be little incentive for writers, artists, sculptors, composers, musicians and a host of other creators to continue their activities. Creators should be able to create, secure in the knowledge that their work is protected against unauthorized use, and that they are free to negotiate a fair financial reward for their work. Absence or abuse of the copyright framework will undermine these inherent rights of the creator and also provide little incentive for those industries who deal in intellectual property to invest in that creativity.

Why then is copyright sometimes regarded as an obstacle to those who wish to utilize and benefit from those creative works? There are a number of situations in which this accusation is made; it has been a particularly common argument in the field of literary works, above all those which are required for educational and academic purposes. In other words, it is often presented as a barrier to the free flow of information.

At the most extreme end of the scale we have seen the situation in a country such as the People's Republic of China, which until June 1st 1991 had no domestic copyright legislation to cover the works of its own creators; it remained outside membership of the Berne Convention and the Universal Copyright Convention until October 1992 when it acceded to both conventions. This followed years of international pressure and the eventual threat of withdrawal of China's most favored nation status by the United States. The reasons for China's long absence from the international copyright community were a mixture of political beliefs and expediency; on an ideological level, the view of copyright as a personal property right was alien to the socialist philosophy. On a more practical level, absence from the conventions gave China many years of free access to foreign works without permission or payment.

Although works of fiction were undoubtedly utilized in this way, there was very extensive use of works such as scientific books and journals and in particular language teaching materials and dictionaries with English as a prime target. Such editions were often hard to track–known as *neibu* or 'internal' editions, they were sold on floors of bookshops which foreigners were not permitted to enter. The print run for an unauthorized local reprint edition of a well-known English language course could easily be several hundred thousand copies, and there were many examples of multiple editions by different publishers, bringing the overall quantities into millions. There were powerful lobbies (in particular from the academic community) against membership of the conventions, but eventually pressure from major trading partners and the increasing unauthorized use of Chinese works within China itself led to the introduction of domestic legislation and accession to the conventions.

Compulsory Licensing

One of the most frequent arguments against copyright—or perhaps more accurately against copyright formalities and the requirement for remuneration to the rights owner—has been from the 'North-South' lobby. This has been voiced frequently by the developing countries, who have long held that their access to educational and academic works from the more affluent countries has been made slower and more difficult or precluded altogether by the requirements of the copyright holders. It was pressure from this lobby which led to the introduction of the 1971 Paris Revisions to the Berne Convention and the Universal Copyright Convention; these made provision for the granting of compulsory reprint or translation licenses for books needed for educational purposes in member states which have claimed official status as developing countries.

Under the Paris Revisions, a number of procedures must be followed before a compulsory license can be awarded, including the requirement that a specified period of time should have elapsed since publication of the original edition and that the applicant makes every effort to contact the foreign rights holder to try and negotiate a voluntary license arrangement. Compulsory licenses may only be granted if the copyright holder cannot be located, fails to reply to the application within a designated period of time, or if a license is refused without adequate reason. Specified periods must have elapsed following first publication of the original publisher's edition before a compulsory translation or reprint license can be requested.

Over the years, there have been many complaints from publishers in the developing countries that despite the provisions of Paris their access to educational and academic books has been impeded, although it is difficult to find statistics which support this argument. Certainly the introduction of the Paris Revisions - and the fact that a number of countries have introduced compulsory licensing into their own domestic copyright legislation, some in line with Paris and some not - has led to a significantly larger number of licenses being granted to publishers in developing countries. One must however ask if this is really the best way to provide educational books to the countries concerned.

No western publisher familiar with the markets concerned would doubt that there is a widening gap between the prices of the original publisher's editions and the purchasing power in the countries concerned. This reflects rising production costs and the raising of the purchase price threshold in more affluent countries. However, the request to pass rights under the threat of a compulsory license is not perhaps the optimum way in which to encourage western publishers to assist with the problem. It is perhaps significant that virtually no license application for an educational or academic book is ever for a new title still in its first edition—applications are above all for books which have been established over the years through export sales of the original publisher's edition through many successive revised editions. Any local licensee therefore has a ready-made market with minimal need for investment in promotion to publicize the book—he is already acquiring a known product.

The Implications of Granting Licenses

Let us look at the implications of granting licenses for books in this way. If the license is for a local low-cost English language reprint edition, the original publisher must accept that once the licensed edition appears, his own edition will no longer have a market in the country concerned. If the same well-established textbook is required for local reprinting in a range of markets such as India, Pakistan, Indonesia, Taiwan, and the Philippines, there will inevitably be a significant impact on export sales of the original edition, particularly for British publishers who have traditionally exported a substantial proportion of their print runs to export markets. The loss of these markets will eventually reduce the overall print run of the original edition, driving up the price still further - and yet there is still an expectation that the western publisher will continue to invest in launching, establishing and maintaining the flow of high quality new books. Even if a translation license is granted, the sale of rights in a major language such as Hindi can have a significant impact on sales of the English edition of the book in India.

What benefits do the author and the original publisher gain from licensing rights? The knowledge that the book will be available in a low-cost English edition or in the local language, certainly; some financial return if all goes well. Equally certain is the loss of sales of the original edition to that market, and probably a minimal financial return from the license; there is a frequent expectation on the part of potential licensees that rights should be passed at a concessionary royalty rate or even totally free of charge. Local bank regulations may mean that the level of advance payment and royalty percentage paid to the licensor are subject to restrictions. Even a higher number of sales of the licensed edition will probably not compensate for the loss of a lower number of direct sales of the original edition, as royalties from the license will normally be based on a very low local price. It is a sad fact that income from licenses of this kind often does not cover even the cost of the paperwork involved in contracting and administering the license and therefore represents an overall (and sometimes substantial) loss to the original publisher.

There are other implications inherent in granting licenses, in particular for local English language reprint rights. The quality of production of the licensed edition is frequently very low and whilst in many countries it would be quite unreasonable to expect production quality comparable to that of the original edition, a poorly produced edition can have a detrimental effect on the reputation of the author and the original publisher and may greatly reduce the usefulness of the book to the end user. This presents a particular problem if the book in question is dependent on many illustrations, e.g., a medical textbook; yet it is precisely books of this kind where the purchase of a set of duplicate printing film can prove too expensive for the licensee. Even if film is purchased, poor quality paper, printing and binding facilities can lead to an unsatisfactory end result. A further problem is that there are frequent instances of local reprint editions 'leaking' outside their designated licensed territory into other markets where they under-cut sales of the original edition or another licensed edition.

Alternatives to Licensing

In the area of academic textbooks, there are alternative methods of supply to the developing countries which do not involve licensing. The British government provides a subsidy to publishers to produce low cost editions of selected student textbooks for developing countries under its Educational Low Cost Books Scheme (ELBS) and the United States Information Agency has a similar scheme for American textbooks in designated subject areas. The ELBS scheme enables British publishers to produce editions in a distinctive livery for sale at approximately one-third of the price of the standard edition. Since funding for schemes of this kind is limited, a number of multinational publishers have long produced their own International Student Editions (ISEs) which are sold to developing countries at prices considerably lower than those of the original editions. In both cases manufacture is maintained under the control of the original publisher, thus ensuring control of production quality and print quantities. The return to both author and publisher on these editions will of course be lower.

Should the Developing Countries Depend on Books from Abroad?

Perhaps the most significant point is that continuing dependence on books from the more affluent countries—whether acquired through licensing or via a low-cost book scheme - does little to encourage the entrepreneurial spirit of the local publishing industries in the countries concerned. The majority of developing countries still maintain the provision of textbooks under state control, but even then tenders are often sought for foreign publishers to supply government contracts. If there is continuing reliance on books from outside, there will be little incentive for local authors and publishers to create and establish their own books to fulfill local market needs.

It is therefore vital for local authors and publishers to seek to develop and improve their own skills to enable them to produce their own books tailored specifically to meet local needs, particularly in the educational sector. There have been numerous initiatives designed to assist with this aim - publishing training courses funded by the World Bank and run locally in the countries concerned with the assistance of publishing consultants from abroad, copyright and licensing courses run by organizations such as WIPO (World Intellectual Property Organization) and UNESCO; national initiatives such as training courses funded by the British Council, the Publishers Association of Great Britain, the Association of American Publishers. the German *Borsenverein* and the French *Syndicat National d'Edition*. There have also been a number of attachment schemes enabling authors and publishing staff from the developing countries to spend several weeks or months working with an individual Western publishing house to see how projects are commissioned and developed, designed and produced, and to see how the work of teams of authors working on large educational projects is coordinated.

In addition to this, some of the larger Western academic and educational publishing houses have invested staff, time and considerable finance in designing new educational materials for specific developing countries, usually working with local educational advisors, authors and often in tandem with local publishing houses; my own house has a publishing division specializing in this type of work with particular experience in the African countries, the Caribbean, mainland China, and increasingly the countries of Central and Eastern Europe. In an ideal world, specially designed materials of this kind with substantial local input must be preferable to licenses of existing material which was designed primarily for other markets.

In the meantime, while the demand persists, educational and academic publishers in the more affluent countries must try to respond to the need for low-cost book supply. It is however crucial that (if licensing is the chosen method) the original publishers can negotiate a fair return for the use of publications in which they and their authors have invested expertise, years of work, and substantial finance. Licensing terms should be tailored to take into account circumstances in the country of the licensee, but a demand for rights to be passed free of charge or for a minimal royalty percentage which may also be based on a minimal local price fails to recognize the intrinsic worth of the title. This can be particularly galling to the original publisher in the case of a request for local reprint rights where the licensee will not have to undertake any investment in editorial work; the costs incurred will simply be those of physical reproduction of an already well-established work. Many licenses are granted to publishers in the developing countries, but the financial implications for the authors and the original publishers are perhaps not fully appreciated by the publishers applying for those rights. It is often forgotten that it is not the designated role of commercial publishers in the more affluent countries to provide aid to less fortunate countries; that should be the role of governments through initiatives such as translation subsidy schemes or low-cost books programs such as ELBS.

The passage of rights in traditional book form between these markets has been a long-running saga which occasionally comes to a head in cases of gross abuse of the rights of copyright owners in countries such as the Philippines and Pakistan, both of which belong to the Berne Convention and the Universal Copyright Convention, and which also benefit from subsidy schemes such as ELBS; nevertheless they continue to maintain compulsory licensing policies which bear no resemblance to the provisions of the Paris

Revisions to the conventions. In the case of the Philippines there are cases of compulsory licenses being granted for books which the original publisher had already made available to the market in a low cost edition; it must then be arguable whether a country with such legislation should continue to benefit from low cost schemes, particularly if they are funded by foreign governments; or indeed whether they should continue in membership of the international conventions when their domestic compulsory licensing provisions are so draconian.

China: the Aftermath of Accession

It will also be interesting to see how matters develop in China. In the experience of many educational and academic publishers since that country's accession to the copyright conventions in October 1992, many Chinese publishers and academic institutes are continuing to reprint or translate foreign titles but are refusing to pay for the rights on the grounds that publication of specialized titles is not profitable and that they have no access to hard currency. In many cases they also refuse to consider making even a modest payment in blocked currency, which can be acceptable to Western publishers who have the opportunity to visit China and collect and utilize such payment. There is strong and continuing evidence that some titles in the area of English language teaching are still being reprinted on a vast scale without permission or payment, often in multiple different editions.

I myself frequently receive applications from individual Chinese translators who may have spent years translating a book before they approach the copyright holder for permission to do so. In some cases they have been translating a long out of date edition; in others, they are themselves paying substantial sums to a Chinese publishing house to cover the cost of producing the translated edition. The publisher often refuses to pay even a token amount in recognition of the rights of the author or the original publisher and may try to place the onus on the translator. There are frequent situations where the Chinese publisher will refuse to proceed with publication of the translation, if the translator cannot reach agreement with the original publisher for the rights; this seems to be a rather backhanded recognition of copyright obligations since the onus for payment should not of course fall on an individual translator. This can lead to distressing situations and yet for the author and the original publisher to agree to grant rights free of charge simply reinforces the old Chinese view that foreign works should be available without payment. Until there is clearer understanding of the moral as well as the legal implications of copyright recognition and the Chinese government puts into place some source of funding for translations of books of this kind, the effect of China's accession to the conventions in 1992 will be minimal.

Erosion of Copyright Protection in the Former Eastern Bloc

Ironically, publishers also face an erosion of their rights in other markets which were once tightly controlled under communist regimes. In the past, licensing to the countries of Central and Eastern Europe and the Soviet Union was conducted via state copyright agencies and licenses were all state-owned publishing houses. The removal of the monopoly of those agencies, an explosion of private publishing houses in all the countries of the region and the removal of the state monopoly on the printing industry have led to the growth of private enterprise, some of it legitimate but much of it based on the piracy of Western books both in translation and reprinted in the original language. The breakup of countries such as the Soviet Union, Czechoslovakia and Yugoslavia into independent states has meant that there is a pressing need to introduce new domestic copyright legislation and to accede to one or both of the conventions; however, revision of intellectual property legislation is, not always high on the agenda of countries facing a range of economic and political problems. Some countries have drafted revised legislation (Poland and Romania); Russia, which inherited the Soviet Union's membership of the Universal Copyright Convention, introduced a new domestic copyright law in mid-1993 as a prelude to applying to join the Berne Convention. All this new legislation now makes provision for action in the case of copyright infringement under both civil and criminal law; these provisions had not been necessary while the publishing and printing industries remained under state control. It is likely that it will be necessary to reinforce the legislation with a number of test cases.

New Technologies: Implications for Copyright Protection

Thus far, I have looked at areas of traditional publishing where the perception of copyright obligations may often differ between copyright owners and would-be users of copyright material. Let me now turn to an area where copyright obligations are also a cause for concern, that of electronic publishing.

The buzzword for the early 1990s has been that of the information superhighway and we are told that by the year 2000, the majority of countries in the world will be linked by supranational electronic networks which will provide us with telecommunications, television and access to information and entertainment on demand. The speed at which sectors of the electronic industry have moved has been daunting, and in the last few years alliances have been formed between industries not hitherto in contact with each other telecommunications, satellite providers, terrestrial broadcasters, electronics manufacturers and media producers such as the film industry, the music industry and publishers. Strategic alliances are being formed in order to take advantage of future multimedia technologies.

Such developments are of course more apparent in the more affluent countries, but already problems are starting to emerge in terms of control over the use of copyright material and how mechanisms can be applied to ensure that copyright owners can trace usage and receive an appropriate financial return.

Photocopying: the First Challenge

At the earliest stage, it was not immediately apparent what impact the development of new technologies would have on the use of copyright material. In the 1950s, nobody envisaged that by the 1970s, large sectors of the population would have ready access to photocopying machines or the scale of photocopying of printed material which would be undertaken. The publishing industries in countries such as the United Kingdom and the United States were slow to grasp the implications of the phenomenon, and it was not until the 1980s that mechanisms were introduced in the form of central licensing agencies to try and control the problem. In the United Kingdom this meant negotiations between the Copyright Licensing Agency (CLA) and a range of different sectors—the local education authorities controlling the state school sector, independent schools, universities and colleges, government departments and private industry, in particular, with sectors such as the pharmaceutical industry. It was estimated that in 1992, copying in the U.K. school sector alone totaled approximately 400 million pages copied. Authors and publishers now receive payment via the licensing agencies for the right to photocopy limited amounts of copyright material; over 10 million pounds has been paid out to U.K. copyright holders since the inception of the scheme.

In the United States, the Copyright Clearance Center (CCC) undertakes a similar role and there are now Reprographic Rights Organizations (RROs) in most European countries. However, not all countries have schemes of this kind and even Japan did not establish one until the early 1990s. One thing is sure: as access to photocopying machines increases in a given country, the copying problem will escalate and measures must be taken to protect the interests of rights owners. In the former communist countries, photocopying machines were relatively few and far between and were kept under lock and key in offices since they could be used for *samizdat* publishing. Now copyshops proliferate and it is frequently Western educational material which is being copied. Mechanisms to deal with the problem could well become one of the roles of the former state copyright agencies, which still exist in the countries concerned but with their monopoly over international rights trading removed.

New Forms of Reprography

Although photocopying continues, it now seems quite a primitive form of reproducing material in the more affluent countries. As technologies have developed, it has become possible to scan and store material in electronic form on computers; the reproduction process may therefore be in ephemeral form on a computer screen through transmission on a network, or via printing off in hard copy form. All of this can take place without the knowledge of the copyright holder. Electrocopying of this kind will pose a serious threat to authors and publishers, unless it can be controlled; in the United Kingdom there are proposals that it should be centrally controlled via the Copyright Licensing Agency as for photocopying; but the type and scale of usage (e.g., by pharmaceutical companies) are such that publishers are more likely to wish to deal with it themselves.

Electrocopying presents an additional problem in, that text stored in this way can be rearranged, manipulated, edited and added to, all of which pose threats to the author's right of integrity, i.e., the right not to have his or her work subjected to derogatory treatment. There is also the danger of infringing the author's right of paternity (the right to be recognized as the author of the work) if parts of a work are incorporated into a larger electronic database without adequate acknowledgment to the original source. These aspects of an author's moral rights are a feature of copyright legislation in the United Kingdom and many European countries although they do not currently feature in US copyright legislation.

Network Publishing, Electronic Libraries and Document Delivery

Areas of particular concern are those of network publishing, electronic libraries and document delivery. Network publishing has been developed very rapidly in the academic sector as an extension of communication within campuses via E-mail. British university campuses are now linked via an electronic network called JANET (Joint Academic Network) and this is now being enhanced into the far more powerful broadband medium of SuperJANET which will permit sound and graphics to be transmitted in addition to text. It is a short step for academics communicating with each other by electronic means on matters of mutual interest, to material being 'published' on the network and bypassing publishers altogether.

There is also a move towards the electronic library, where books and journals are scanned and stored electronically and can then be viewed through networked workstations, usually with facilities to download and print off material as hard copy. A number of experimental projects of this kind are under way in the United States, Columbia University Law School, the Kent Law Library of the University of Illinois and Carnegie Mellon University are all working in this field whilst in the United Kingdom an experimental electronic information on-line retrieval project (ELINOR) has been established at De Montfort University; publishers have licensed fifty books in the field of business information to be included for access via terminals. In each case the experiments are monitoring facilities to trace access and log payment due to copyright holders.

In the United Kingdom the prospect of an even larger electronic library looms. SuperJANET links not only university campuses but also includes institutes such as the British Library, which has stated its intention to make its holding electronically available by the year 2000. Combine this with a facility to transmit copies of copyright material electronically to users and the scale of the potential threat to publishers as information providers and as guardians of copyright material becomes apparent, with the additional irony that British publishers are required to provide one deposit copy of everything they publish free of charge to the British Library.

The British Library Document Supply Center (BLDSC) already provides a document delivery service in hard copy form to academic institutes and commercial users. It has been estimated that more than three million documents a year were supplied in this way to customers in the United Kingdom and abroad, initially without any payment to copyright holders because of the special dispensation for libraries to provide single copies of copyright material for research purposes free of charge; yet many documents were being supplied to companies such as the pharmaceutical industry for commercial rather than for private or academic research.

There is now an agreement between BLDSC and the British Copyright Licensing Agency (CLA) to pay a fee for the supply of individual Journal articles at a rate of £2 per article copied. However, BLDSC is now seeking to extend the arrangement to cover the supply of material electronically to customers worldwide, a facility already provided by a number of commercial document delivery services. The document delivery service is currently estimated to be worth about £50 million and rising fast, yet only a very small proportion of this money finds its way to the original producer of the works which are being copied.

The provision of selected copyright material on demand in this way is likely to reinforce the trend for libraries and commercial organizations such as the drug companies to cease to subscribe to academic journals in traditional paper form altogether and instead to order individual articles on demand from indexing services available to them from commercial companies such as Uncover and Faxon. At present, most document supply is in traditional paper form or by fax for an additional charge, but there is an increasing move toward electronic document delivery with the subscriber printing off hard copy at the point of receipt. In the meantime, journal subscriptions have been falling by approximately 5% per year since 1990; publishers must seriously question whether they should continue to produce journals in traditional print-on-paper form and consider instead providing electronic delivery of their own material direct to customer, rather than via third parties. A number of such experiments are already being conducted either by individual major journal publishers such as Elsevier or by groups of like-minded journal publishers.

The inherent difficulty in controlling the use of copyright material may be envisaged when one looks at Internet, an electronic network originally set up by U.S. federal research bodies to enable them to communicate with each other on matters of interest. Internet has grown on an ad hoc basis and is now a supranational telecommunications system which currently links approximately 11,000 private and public networks in over 125 countries, covering 1.5 million host computers and over 20 million individual users. It provides gateways into a wide range of copyright databases and the fact that it is so wide-ranging has led its users to expect to have access to substantial amounts of information free of charge. It is therefore vital from the point of view of authors and publishers that some means are found to track the usage of copyright material via the electronic media and to build in a 'metering' mechanism to facilitate payment for such use.

Is the Book Finally Dead?

Much has been made in the last few years of the impending death of the traditional book in favor of publishing in a variety of electronic forms, ranging from straightforward publication of text through the media of on-line databases or CD-ROM, multimedia publications incorporating text, graphics, sound, music and interactive facilities on CD-ROM, CD—I or on hand-held electronic products such as SONY Data Discman. While publishers must undoubtedly pay serious attention to these new media—and they may indeed be an ideal alternative for encyclopedias and illustrated information books in the more affluent markets - the fact remains that in many situations the traditional book is the ideal medium to provide both information and pleasure. It is a more acceptable medium for long periods of reading, whether for study or for enjoyment; it offers portability without the need for renewal of batteries and probably has no rival in encouraging the sheer imaginative powers of the user. Who wants to curl up in bed with a Data Discman?

From the publisher's point of view, the electronic revolution is both a threat and an opportunity. We may choose to license our materials for use in this form, or take the plunge and enter the market ourselves, either developing our own product or entering into partnerships with electronic producers. It has been estimated that by the year 2000, British publishers will be deriving between 10% and 30% of their income from publishing in non-traditional media.

Copyright Protection is Even More Vital for the Future

The impact of the new technologies on copyright must not however be underestimated. If copyright material is to form the basis of new products, or is to be transmitted via electronic networks which transcend geographical borders, tracking and payment mechanisms must be introduced to 'record and reward.' Work is already being carried out on encryption which would restrict access to material to authorized users and also log what is accessed in order to calculate payment due to the copyright holder.

We cannot afford to ignore the future but neither can we afford to ignore the importance of copyright as a means of ensuring a fair reward both for creators themselves, and for those industries who invest in creativity by bringing 'works of the mind' into tangible form. Recognition of copyright obligations by users of sophisticated technology is just as important as recognition by users of books in the less affluent countries. It would be ironic to see the importance of copyright eroded by the new technologies just as the last remaining countries in the world are being persuaded to join the international conventions. It is vital that domestic copyright legislation is constantly reviewed to take into account the implications of technological developments—for example, many laws do not yet afford specific copyright protection to computer programs or video recordings, both of which are highly vulnerable to unauthorized copying with highly damaging results for the industries concerned.

In our own book industry, we do not wish to impede access to information; provision of information is after all the prime reason for business for many of us. However, we must ensure that legislation and administrative mechanisms are in place to guarantee a fair return for that use, and this applies equally whether the users are school pupils or university students in developing countries, or whether they are academics or researchers wishing to access information via an electronic network. The size and nature of the payment must be tailored to match the circumstances but uncontrolled and free access to information without recognition of the input of authors and publishers can only be detrimental in the long term.

CONTRIBUTORS

Philip G. Altbach is professor of higher education at Boston College, and is director of the Research and Information Center of the Bellagio Publishing Network. He is author of *The Knowledge Context: Comparative Perspectives on the Distribution of Knowledge* and editor of *Publishing and Development in the Third World*. Most recently, he co-edited (with Edith S. Hoshino) *International Book Publishing: An Encyclopedia*.

Urvashi Butalia is on the staff of Kali for Women, a feminist publisher located in New Delhi, India. She is currently preparing a study on women's publishing in the Third World for the Bellagio Publishing Network. She has written for *Logos* and other journals.

Henry Chakava is managing director of East African Educational Publishers, Ltd., Nairobi, Kenya. He is a board member of the African Publishers Network and of the African Books Collective. One of Africa's most respected publishers, Mr. Chakava worked with UNESCO and other international agencies.

Dina Nath Malhotra is chairman of Hind Pocket Books, Ltd., New Delhi, India. He pioneered the mass paperback in India. Mr. Malhotra has been president of Federation of Indian Publishers on several occasions and is currently chair of the Copyright Council of the FIP. He has been a consultant to UNESCO and other international agencies.

Lynette Owen started her publishing career with Cambridge University Press, and is currently Rights and Contracts Director for the Longman Group, where she has worked since 1976. She is author of *Selling Rights, Second Edition*, and has run training courses in Greece, Malaysia, China and other countries.

Janice Wickeri is Managing Editor of *Renditions*, a Chinese-English translation magazine published in Hong Kong, where she has lived for the past decade. She has published numerous translations of Chinese literature and theological writings, the latter for *The Chinese Theological Review*, which she also edits.

SOCIAL SCIENCE LIBRARY

Oxford University Library Services
Manor Road
Oxford OX1 3UQ
Tel: (2)71093 (enquiries and renewals)
http://www.ssl.ox.ac.uk

This is a NORMAL LOAN item.

We will email you a reminder before this item is due.

Please see http://www.ssl.ox.ac.uk/lending.html
for details on:

- loan policies; these are also displayed on the notice boards and in our library guide.

- how to check when your books are due back.

- how to renew your books, including information on the maximum number of renewals. Items may be renewed if not reserved by another reader. Items must be renewed before the library closes on the due date.

- level of fines; fines are charged on overdue books.

Please note that this item may be recalled during Term.